THE WAY OF

ALOHA
—MOLOKA'I—

THE WAY OF

ALOHA

—MOLOKA'I—

pehea ka lā?

CAMERON C. TAYLOR

Books by Cameron C. Taylor

8 Attributes of Great Achievers

8 Attributes of Great Achievers, Volume II

Preserve, Protect, & Defend

Does Your Bag Have Holes? 24 Truths That Lead to Financial and Spiritual Freedom

Twelve Paradoxes of the Gospel

8 Steps to Lasting Excellence

The Way of Aloha: Lana'i

Author's Website
www.CameronCTaylor.com

Library of Congress Control Number: 2019903913
ISBN-13: 978-0-9796861-7-7
Printed in the United States of America

This dedication was written shortly after I learned of the death of my friend, Mitch Huhem, on February 23, 2016.

This book is dedicated to Mitch Huhem, my friend, my mentor, my kahuna (expert), and my kumu (teacher). I learned from him how to be an instrument in the hands of the Lord in business and in life. He is a man full of love, generosity, happiness, and vision. He often told me, "I love you," both in letters and in person—even in business settings where this is all too rare. I love you too, Mitch. I miss you, brother. Oh, how I miss you.

Mitch, your positive influence continues in my life and the lives of my children. I will be eternally grateful for your love, example, generosity, life, and your faith in me. As you know, my oldest son is named after you. I hope he grows up to become like the Mitch Huhem I know—the mighty man of God who I'm blessed to call my friend. I love you, Mitch. Aloha and mahalo nui loa!

Friendships are eternal. We will always be connected, even when we're not in the same physical location. God be with you till we meet again. A hui hou.

CONTENTS

Hawaiian Pronunciation Guide	9
Preface	10
Chapter 1: Aloha	16
Chapter 2: Kuleana	24
Chapter 3: Asking for Permission	32
Chapter 4: Rubbing Shoulders with Christ	38
Chapter 5: Slow Down	46
Chapter 6: Hālawa Valley	58
Chapter 7: Dinner with Naniwaiwai	66
Chapter 8: The Profound Principles of Poi	74
Chapter 9: Hālawa Bay	86
Chapter 10: ʻAumākua	100
Chapter 11: Moʻoula Falls	112
Chapter 12: Hike to Mountain Heiau	124
Chapter 13: You Can Do All Things	138
Chapter 14: Mana	150
Chapter 15: Kapuaiwa Royal Coconut Grove	170
Chapter 16: Kamakou Mountain	184
Chapter 17: Kalaupapa	202
Chapter 18: The Pū Hala Tree	216
Chapter 19: The Cove at Kalawao	230

Chapter 20: Saint Philomena Church   236

Chapter 21: Kalaupapa Bookstore   248

Chapter 22: Monuments   260

Chapter 23: Family Reunion   276

Chapter 24: Flight Home   282

Epilogue   288

Acknowledgments   290

About the Author   291

Endnotes   292

HAWAIIAN
PRONUNCIATION GUIDE

The Hawaiian alphabet consists of thirteen letters:

Five vowels (a, e, i, o, u)

Eight consonants (h, k, l, m, n, p, w, ʻokina)

The ʻokina is a reversed apostrophe used as a glottal stop.

Vowel Pronunciations:

"a" is pronounced like "a" in father

"e" is pronounced like "ey" in they

"i" is pronounced like "ee" in see

"o" is pronounced like "o" in no

"u" is pronounced like "oo" in too

"ai" or "ae" is pronounced like the "i" in ride

"ao" is pronounced like the "ow" in how

"au" is pronounced like the "ou" in loud

"ei" is pronounced as the "ei" in eight

"oi" or "oe" is pronounced like the "oy" in boy

"ou" is pronounced like the "ow" in bowl

"ui" is pronounced like the "ooey" in gooey

"eu" is pronounced: eh-(y)oo

"iu" is pronounced: ee-(y)oo

Consonant Pronunciations:

All of the consonants are pronounced the same as in English, except the w, which is usually pronounced as a "v" after a, i or e. W is pronounced as a "w" at the beginning of a word, or after o or u.

PREFACE

"I do not think there is a better place in the kingdom of man, than the Island of Moloka'i. These people are truly blessed... They have large farms, fruit trees, taro patches, and much fish... The people [are] so prosperous... The view is splendid, the climate ideal." [1]

- Statement by 1880 census taker

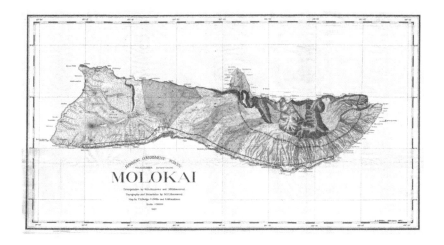

Bible Translations

I reference different versions of the Bible because the study of various translations can give insight into the meaning of the original text. The original text of the Bible contains 11,280 unique words in Hebrew, Aramaic, and Greek. The English translations of the Bible only contain about 6,000 unique words. For example, in the New Testament, there are seven different Greek words with slightly different meanings that are all translated into the single English word "servant."

Exodus 20:13 provides an example. The King James Version reads, "Thou shalt not kill." This translation would appear to exclude all killing, including self-defense and war. The Hebrew word used to describe all forms of killing is the word "harag." The Hebrew word in Exodus 20:13 is "ratsah," which refers to acts of criminal killing. So, a more accurate translation of Exodus 20:13 might be, "Thou shalt not murder."[2] Looking at various translations of Exodus 20:13 that translate "ratsah" as "murder" instead of "kill" can provide greater understanding of the Hebrew word used in Exodus 20:13. The New International Version, New Living Translation, English Standard Version, New American Standard Bible, and many others translate Exodus 20:13 to be "Thou shalt not murder" instead of "Thou shalt not kill."

My family and I are learning the Hawaiian language together from a *kumu* in Hawai'i. The word *kumu* is often translated as "teacher" in English, but if you asked a Hawaiian to define *kumu* and a person in Utah to define teacher, you would get very different answers. The same is true for the Hawaiian word *hālau*. *Hālau* is often translated as "school," but the Hawaiian way of learning and the mainland way of learning are extremely different. Much of the meaning of the word *hālau* is changed when the English word school is used.

In our first Hawaiian lesson, we were taught that you cannot understand the language without understanding the Hawaiian culture, history, and stories. To become fluent, you have to become Hawaiian. Hawaiian is a verb, not a noun. It's a way of life, a way of thinking. To be fluent in Hawaiian requires a deep understanding that's more a function of the Spirit, heart, spiritual eyes, and spiritual ears than the physical mind, eyes, and ears. To speak Hawaiian, you must live by the spirit of Aloha.

Hawaiian words have layers of meaning. Their words are like parables. Much is lost in the translation to English. For example, "*Aloha 'āina*" is often translated to English as "love of the land," but as with all Hawaiian words, the definition cannot be captured with a few words of translation. The phrase *Aloha 'āina* is a connection with God and His creations. Nature is a great gift from our Creator and is much more than physical objects. *'Āina* is filled with *mana* (spiritual power), spirit, and breath (life). *'Āina* is sacred and nourishes our body and spirit. There is much more meaning to the phrase "*Aloha 'āina*" than is captured in the English translation "love of the land."

Just as meaning can be lost or changed going from Hawaiian to English, so, too, can meaning be lost or changed when the original Biblical languages of Hebrew, Aramaic, and Greek are translated to English. Looking at the Hebrew, Aramaic, and Greek words of the Bible, along with various English translations, can help us better understand the meanings of various scriptures.

Additionally, viewing other translations can help us see a familiar scripture in a new light, revealing a deeper and/or alternative meaning. We may think we know what a verse is saying because we have heard it many times. A new translation of a familiar scripture can be a catalyst for deeper thought and understanding. "Blessed are your eyes, for they see: and your ears, for they hear."[3]

Who are you to write books on the ancient principles of Aloha?

I have made multiple trips to Moloka'i to learn from the people and places of this sacred island. As my wife, Paula, and I prepared for one of our trips to Moloka'i, I pondered on the places we should visit and the people we should meet. One individual I felt I should visit was Aunty Teri, the owner of Kalele Bookstore & Divine Expressions in Kaunakakai. The morning after we arrived on Moloka'i, we stopped at the bookstore and were warmly greeted by Aunty Teri. She radiated hospitality, love, and warmth. It was wonderful talking with her. I asked her about various places we wanted to visit on the island.

My questions were not those of a typical tourist, and she asked, "What's your interest in these sacred places?"

I answered, "I'm working on a book on Molokaʻi and the ancient principles of Aloha."

Surprise and doubt overtook her body language as she replied, "Who are you to write a book on Molokaʻi?"

I answered with my favorite scripture, "I can do all things through Christ who strengthens me."[4]

My response didn't deter her skepticism. She shook her head and said, "I don't think you will get much support from the island *kūpuna* [elders]."

While she had her doubts about my writing a book, she was extremely helpful and welcoming. We continued to talk on various topics, and Paula and I purchased several items, including a few books on Molokaʻi that she recommended.

As I left the bookstore, I pondered Aunty Teri's question, "Who am I to write on ancient Hawaiian history, practices, and principles?"

As I thought about this question, these words from the Lord came to my mind, "For unto this end have I raised you up, that I might show forth my wisdom through the weak things of the earth.[5] I call upon the weak things of the world, those who are unlearned and despised.[6] For the Lord's errand...the weak shall confound the wise.[7] Aloha will change the world."

As I wrote about this experience from Molokaʻi, these words from President Russell M. Nelson, a prophet and apostle of the Lord

Jesus Christ, came to my mind, "The Lord has more in mind for you than you have in mind for yourself! As you love Him and keep His commandments, great rewards—even unimaginable achievements—may be yours… The Lord uses the unlikely to accomplish the impossible!… As a Latter-day Saint, you…can accomplish the impossible. You can help shape the destiny of the human family!… You can change the world."[8]

We look back on Biblical events and on certain periods of history, and we see great wonders that God performed at the hands of people we call "the giants of the faith." But the only real giant in the picture is God, and He hasn't changed. He used absolutely ordinary people then, and He will do the same today.[9]

Is Manu Nāpela real?

While Manu is a fictional character, he is also real. I have had a hard time describing this. Manu represents the wisdom and experience of several real people. I have been taught many things by the *kūpuna* of Moloka'i. As I have pondered and prayed at the sacred places of Moloka'i, I have been taught things by Hawaiian angels, the Lord Jesus Christ, and the Holy Spirit. Manu represents the Hawaiian *kūpuna*, the Hawaiian angels, the Lord Jesus Christ, and the Holy Spirit—all of whom are very real.

CHAPTER 1
ALOHA

"Aloha is my favorite word because when you say it, it makes everyone smile."

- Makoa, age 5

808. Who could be calling me from Hawaiʻi? I wondered. Although I didn't recognize the phone number, 808 was definitely the Hawaiʻi area code. I answered the call, "Aloha, this is Cameron."

A loud and lengthy "*A-lo-ha!*" boomed through the receiver. I recognized the voice immediately. It was Manu Nāpela. Excitement and happiness flooded over me.

"Manu," I couldn't stop smiling, "It's so good to hear your voice."

"It's nice to hear your voice as well, Elder Taylor, or should I say Cameron C. Taylor? I've read your book several times. It has brought back so many wonderful memories and feelings. Your book has created quite a stir of excitement. It seems that everyone I run into has read it. I'm getting asked a lot of questions. We've even seen an increase in visitors to Lanaʻi as people want to see the sights you talk about in the book. In fact, there are people doing *The Way of Aloha* tours to the sites mentioned in your book. I even have people stopping by my home on occasion. One of my kids called me after reading the book and said, 'Dad, I can't believe you're famous.'"

"That's fun to hear." If only he knew how relieved I was to hear that. "I was hoping the book would be well received in Hawai'i, even though it was written by a *haole*." (*Haole* is a Hawaiian word for white people.)

Laughing, Manu replied, "You're no *haole*. You're Hawaiian. Being Hawaiian isn't dependent on where you live, the color of your skin or your genetics. Being Hawaiian is about how you live. Being Hawaiian is a matter of the heart, an attitude, and a state of mind. All who live with Aloha are Hawaiian. Hawaiian isn't a noun. Hawaiian is a verb. You are Hawaiian."

"That's very kind of you to say, Manu. When a form asks for my ethnicity, if Pacific Islander is one of the options, I typically check that box. When the ethnicity is a blank box to fill in, I write Hawaiian. I think of myself as Hawaiian, but I sometimes get strange looks as I greet people in Idaho with a hardy 'Aloha.' While some find it unusual to be greeted with a warm Aloha on a snowy day, I've found there is great *mana* (spiritual power) in the word Aloha. Just saying 'Aloha' brightens the day and lifts the soul."

"Precisely," Manu agreed. "Aloha isn't isolated to Hawai'i. Aloha is to fill the world. Aloha is much more than a word or a greeting. It's a blessing of love, praise, and gratitude. Aloha overflows with generosity, power, abundance, beauty, compassion, and joy. Hawai'i is one of God's sacred creations and Aloha is His way of life. Aloha is the humble acknowledgment of a Divine creator and a desire to live His way. Aloha isn't merely a word or a concept, but a way of life. Aloha isn't place-dependent, unless the place you're referring to is the heart. The spirit of Aloha is the spirit of Christ and it fills the world."

As Manu spoke, the Spirit filled my soul. His love and gentle spirit carried through the phone. "Yes. Aloha is so much more than a word. Our family mission statement is 'Live Aloha,' as Aloha encompasses all the attitudes, attributes, and actions we strive to exemplify. I often tell people I live on the island of Idaho."

Manu chuckled, "Your island has one of the largest beaches in the world—Oregon."

We both laughed and I asked, "When are you going to come and visit the island of Idaho?"

"I would love to visit the island of Idaho," Manu answered, "but I'm calling to invite you to come with me to the island of Molokaʻi. We've been invited to work on a book. I received a call from Naniwaiwai. She is a friend of mine, 107 years young, who I shared *The Way of Aloha: Lanaʻi* with. She called me and recounted a dream she had the night after finishing your book. In that dream, you and I were on the island of Molokaʻi with her working on a book. She saw the homes of her children, grandchildren, and great-grandchildren. Her posterity were reading the Bible, the Book of Mormon, and another book. This other book contained the history, stories, and genealogies of Molokaʻi. As the dream concluded, she saw the three books on a shelf next to each other, and the small book on Molokaʻi faded and disappeared. The disappearing book was a message to her that if she didn't act to preserve and perpetuate the history, stories, and genealogies of her family on Moloka'i, they would fade away and not be available to her children and grandchildren."

As Manu spoke of Naniwaiwai's dream, the Spirit washed over me. Manu continued, "Naniwaiwai said to me, 'We have the books of history, faith-building stories, and genealogies we call the Bible and the Book of Mormon. These books preserve history and build our faith and knowledge.

"'I would like to create a book with the history, stories, and genealogies of Moloka'i to share with my children, grandchildren, and great-grandchildren who are now spread all over the world. I know some will not like a written book as that isn't the ancient Hawaiian way, and some will not like that I'm working with a child from Idaho. My answer to them is that the Hawaiian way is the Lord's way. Should I ignore the prompting of the Holy Spirit and not fulfill this *kuleana* (divine given responsibility)? I believe my life is being extended and preserved until I fulfill this *kuleana* from the Lord to preserve our stories of faith and family.'"

Manu paused momentarily. As he continued, his voice filled with emotion. "Elder Taylor, I've felt this book is also a part of my *kuleana*. It's often said in Hawai'i that you don't choose your *kuleana*. Your *kuleana* chooses you. We've been chosen. The history, stories, and genealogies of Moloka'i have been passed down for thousands of years, but the days of a communal agricultural society have disappeared and so has the process of the *'ohana* (family) preserving and perpetuating these things from generation to generation." He paused and waited before saying, "So, Elder Taylor, what do you think?"

I gathered my thoughts and emotions in silence. Manu didn't speak either, knowing that silence is when the most is spoken. I was surprised and humbled by the request. I felt inadequate to complete such a work. My knowledge of the Hawaiian culture, language, and history was minimal compared to the wisdom possessed by Manu and Naniwaiwai. I wanted to shrink from the assignment but was strengthened as the Lord whispered to me through His Holy Spirit saying, "You can do all things through Christ who strengthens you. The Lord uses the weak and the unlikely to move forth His work and accomplish His purposes." I knew that many of the experiences and opportunities the Lord had given me over the past forty years were preparation to assist in this work. I felt the call and the confidence of the Lord to assist.

I finally broke the silence. "I feel as if I've received a second mission call to serve in Hawai‘i."

Manu laughed. "Yes. That's one way to express it. Looks like our first area of service for this mission is going to be on the island of Moloka‘i."

A bubbling joy made its way to my voice. "You will be the senior companion, right?"

Manu laughed again. "Sure, Elder Taylor. Whatever you say. But remember that you have a gift—a gift given you by God to write, teach, inspire, and lift. I saw this gift in action as I read *The Way of Aloha: Lana‘i*. Naniwaiwai also felt your gift. She spoke of your Aloha, *mana*, and Hawaiian spirit. Much of this work will be directed by you as you take the wisdom that's shared and use your gift of storytelling and your gifts to both teach and be taught by the

Spirit as you preserve, perpetuate, and revive the way of Aloha. You are to be an instrument in the hands of the Lord to write the book."

Tears streamed down my face. I tried to formulate a response, but no words came.

Manu continued, "Naniwaiwai would like us to come to Moloka'i next month when they are having their family reunion."

My silence persisted. Many emotions fought for control— surprise, inadequacy, excitement, and anxiety. Finally, I responded, "I feel the Lord's hand at work. I'll discuss this with my wife and children and give you a call back. I feel the Lord has prepared a way for this to happen."

CHAPTER 2
KULEANA

"Never cease to act because you fear you may fail."

- Queen Liliʻuokalani

Excitement filled the room as we gathered as a family to discuss my phone call with Manu.

"I can't believe Manu invited you to come to Moloka'i," exclaimed my oldest son, Mitchell.

"We get to come with you, right, Dad?" chimed in ten-year-old Kennedy. "We'll help you with your book."

"Please, please, please, Dad." Enoch's pleading hadn't stopped since I'd told him about the phone call. "You and Mom never take us with you to Hawai'i."

Mitchell jumped in, "Yeah, Dad. We've been dying to go since reading your book. It's about time you finally took us."

I really wanted to take the whole family to Moloka'i, but I had a feeling this wasn't the right trip for them to join me.

"You're right, Mitchell. Mom and I do need to take you to Hawai'i. However, I don't think this will be the trip. I feel strongly that it's my *kuleana* to make this particular trip to Moloka'i.

"A cool what?" Enoch was the most inquisitive. Sometimes, his questions were incessant, but I love questions because they are the key to learning.

"A *kuleana*," I replied. "I've often told you that if the Lord needs an errand run, He can ask a Taylor to do it. Right?"

Three heads nodded in agreement.

"And as did the Savior, we want to go about doing good.[10] Correct?" Again, they nodded.

"Well, a *kuleana* is an errand from the Lord to do something good—to do something to make the world a better place. *Kuleana* is an action word meaning to take responsibility that can be described as something you were foreordained to do—a mission, a calling."

"I think it's my *kuleana* to go to Hawai'i," Kennedy replied with a smile.

Laughing, I replied, "I promise we'll go to Hawai'i as a family, but for this trip to Moloka'i, I think it would be best if I go by myself."

Disappointed sighs filled the room. "When will we get to go to Hawai'i then, Dad?" Mitchell didn't try to hide his disappointment.

My wife, Paula, looked at me, and I gave a silent nod of approval. "Dad and I were going to wait until Christmas to tell you about this. We've already bought airline tickets for our entire family to go to Hawai'i next year for several weeks."

Cheers and questions erupted from all three children simultaneously. Kennedy's excitement surged through her body so that she bounced on the balls of her feet. "When are we going?"

Mitchell hid his emotions better, but that didn't stop him from asking the important question, "Can I go surfing?"

With a few more, "What island are we staying on?" and "Will we get to see turtles?" I tried to bring things back to a normal level.

"Slow down, everyone," I said. "We have plenty of time to answer all of your questions later. Right now, I need to make sure I have yours and Mom's blessing to go to Molokaʻi with Manu, and I need to call Manu and let him know our decision."

After consent was given from everyone, Mitchell asked, "Can we be on the call when you talk with Manu, Dad?"

While I'd kept in contact with Manu on occasion through the years, none of my children had ever talked with him personally. After reading about Manu in the book, all of them were eager to talk with him.

"I'm sure Manu would love that," I said. "Let's give him a call." I dialed Manu's number and placed him on speaker phone. Manu answered with his characteristic long and loud, "*A-lo-ha.*" We all laughed upon hearing his joyful greeting.

"Elder Taylor, you're obviously not alone. Who do you have on the phone with you?"

"My children all read *The Way of Aloha: Lanaʻi*," I replied. "They are anxious to hear your voice and to meet you. I'm sure they will want me to have you sign each of their books when I come to Molokaʻi."

The kids nodded their heads in agreement, expressing their desires for Manu to sign their books.

As Manu laughed, he said, "Each of you, tell me your name, your age, and give me your best Aloha, and I promise I'll sign your book."

I pointed to my oldest son for him to begin, "Aloha, Manu. I'm Mitchell and I'm thirteen." He forced calm into his voice, but a nervous tapping of his finger on the table revealed the apprehension underneath.

I pointed to my daughter. "Hi, Manu. My name is Kennedy and I'm ten."

"I didn't hear an Aloha, Kennedy," Manu said.

"Aloha, Manu." She giggled and clasped her hands in front her.

Not one to hold back, Enoch promptly blurted out, "Aloha, Manu. I'm Enoch, and I'm seven."

"It's wonderful to hear each of your voices," said Manu, "and to share Aloha with you. Please always remember that the word Aloha isn't a greeting like hello or good morning. Aloha encompasses all that's good. 'Aloha' should not be taken lightly. 'Aloha' was used anciently as one of the names of God,[11] 'for God is love.'[12] Using the word Aloha inappropriately or frivolously is taking the name of God in vain. Aloha should be said with reverence."

I furiously scribbled notes onto a notepad, not wanting to miss a word. In my haste to record his wisdom, I didn't notice that silence filled the room.

Manu's voice broke my rush of note writing. "Elder Taylor, are you taking notes again?"

Though he couldn't see me, I sheepishly set my pencil down. "You caught me."

Manu laughed and replied, "I'm just teasing you, brother."

As we were laughing, Kennedy asked, "Manu, have your

children said anything funny lately?"

Manu's deep voice softened when he answered her. "Your dad was here as a missionary twenty years ago, so all of my children are now grown."

It was hard to believe that I lived on Lana'i twenty years ago as a young missionary. I left in late March of 1996.

Manu continued, "Kennedy, I do have a funny story for you from my days teaching primary. One Sunday, I asked each child in my class to draw a picture of a Bible story. I watched as the children diligently worked on their pictures. One of the boys had finished his drawing of an airplane with four people aboard. I was very curious what Bible story this could be and asked, 'What Bible story have you drawn?'

"The boy answered, 'This is Mary, Joseph, and Jesus on their flight to Egypt.'"

Only the sound of Manu continuing with his story could quiet my children's laughter. "This accounted for three of the four people on the plane, so I asked, 'Who is the fourth person at the front of plane?'"

"The boy replied, 'That's Pontius, the pilot.'"

Manu's jolly, joyful laugh was contagious, so hearing his laughter made each of us laugh even harder.

"Elder Taylor, I've missed laughing with you. Are you calling to tell me that you're able to come to Moloka'i next month?"

"Yes, Manu. We discussed it as a family," I said, looking again at each of their nodding heads. "And they have given me permission to go."

"Wonderful," exclaimed Manu. "I'm delighted to hear that."

After discussing logistics of the Moloka'i trip for a few minutes, we talked story with Manu. ("Talk story" is a common expression in Hawai'i that means talking with friends, rekindling old times, or informal chatting.)

At the close of the call, Manu said, "It's been fun talking story with you. *A hui hou*, my friends."

Reluctant and staggered responses came from each of my family members. "*A hui hou*, Manu. *A hui hou*."

CHAPTER 3
ASKING FOR PERMISSION

"The best and most beautiful things in the world cannot be seen or even touched. They must be felt with the heart."

- Helen Keller

I searched for a flight to Moloka'i. I decided to fly out of Salt Lake City since the flights out of Idaho Falls were so expensive. After sending my flight details to Manu, he replied with some information to "prepare my heart to receive." A portion of his email read:

"Asking permission is a very important practice of Aloha. All of God's creations are connected to a people and a place. All creations are filled with *ha* (breath of life) and *mana* (spiritual power). The rocks, the trees, the birds are all alive and all can speak. It's very important to request permission before using something or visiting a place. Even in tasks that may seem trivial to some, such as climbing a tree, permission should be sought. You should ask and receive the tree's permission before you climb. Knowledge also belongs to a people and a place and is something that must be requested. Please request and receive the needed permissions prior to your arrival in Moloka'i. Permission must be received from the right person. Asking permission and giving thanks are Aloha principles that should be followed in every aspect of life."

His words and the warmth of the Spirit impressed upon my mind and heart the importance of asking permission. I didn't exactly know who to ask for permission. I turned to prayer, both to know what to pray for and how to ask for permission. I included in my prayer and pondering to know who to ask.

As I prayed and pondered, I was given a vision of Joseph Smith at the Hill Cumorah. I saw Joseph arriving at the place shown to him in a vision and uncovering the gold plates. As Joseph sought to take the plates from the box, he was shocked. Joseph made additional attempts to retrieve the plates and was again shocked and thrown back. "Why can't I receive this book?" Joseph called out in frustration.

The angel Moroni appeared to answer Joseph's questions, telling him that he couldn't receive the plates with thoughts of obtaining the plates to gain wealth or fame. In order to receive the plates, Joseph needed an eye single to the glory of God.

Moroni declared, "If ever these sacred things are obtained, they must be by prayer and faithfulness in obeying the Lord. They are not deposited here for the sake of accumulating gain and wealth for the glory of this world. They were sealed by the prayer of faith and because of the knowledge which they contain. They are of no worth among the children of men, only for their knowledge."[13]

Joseph Smith had to have permission from the angel Moroni before he could receive the gold plates. When he tried to take the plates without permission, he was shocked. I understood that I, too, must receive permission before I would receive Hawaiian knowledge.

After the vision of the Prophet Joseph, I saw Hawaiian angels. It was impressed upon my mind that there are individuals on both sides of the veil who have a *kuleana* to preserve, protect, and share their cultures, languages, histories, and practices. The Bible preserved the language, culture, and stories of Abraham, Moses, Peter, and John. The Book of Mormon preserved the language, culture and stories of Nephi, Alma, Mormon, and Moroni. Just as Moroni was given a *kuleana* to protect and preserve the golden plates and the language, stories, and history of the Nephites, so there are ancient Hawaiian angels who have a *kuleana* to do the same for Hawai'i.

Tears flowed down my cheeks as I saw these angels of Hawai'i. I prayed in gratitude for the many who had lived and served on the islands of Hawai'i—those who recorded and preserved the Hawaiian culture, history, and language. I asked these angels for permission to receive the knowledge, wisdom, and experience contained in their culture. It was impressed upon my mind and heart the sacredness of the records of Hawaiian history, language, and knowledge. My love for the land, the people, and the place grew. I felt the weight of responsibility rest upon my shoulders to preserve, restore, and share the knowledge of Aloha.

I understood that one of the reasons it was vital for me to ask permission was to make sure my motives and intentions were honorable. For my request to be granted, it was essential for me to have an eye single to the glory of God. Asking for permission also gave the angels the opportunity to impress upon my mind and heart the sacred nature of this knowledge and to admonish me that I must receive this knowledge with great care to protect it.

As I asked permission, I felt the door open to the ministering of angels. I sensed Hawaiian angels, filled with love and excitement, gathering around me. They were elated that a portion of the knowledge that had been hidden and preserved for centuries was soon to be shared. These angels gathered around me to give me strength, courage, and confidence. Their presence brought these words of the Lord to my mind, "I will go before your face. I will be on your right hand and on your left, and my Spirit shall be in your hearts, and mine angels round about you, to bear you up."[14]

I was ready to receive.

CHAPTER 4

RUBBING SHOULDERS
WITH CHRIST

"You don't have to tell me about yourself. It's written on your countenance."

- Aunty Margaret Machado

The day of my flight arrived quickly. As I prepared to leave, I exchanged hugs and expressions of love with my wife and each of my children. As I opened the back door to enter the garage, Kennedy ran to me, jumped into my arms, and threw her arms around my neck. "I love you, Daddy." She looked me straight in the eyes. "Are you sure you remembered to bring my book for Manu to sign?"

Each of my children had a copy of *The Way of Aloha: Lana'i* with a personalized note from me in it. I had promised to have Manu add a note of his own.

"Yes, Kennedy, I'm positive. I promise to bring your book back to you with a note from Manu." I placed Kennedy back on the ground and, with a final wave and "I love you," my trip to Moloka'i had officially begun.

The three-hour trip to Salt Lake City passed quickly as I listened to an audio book about Moloka'i. I parked in the long-term parking lot and made my way to the bus that would take me to my terminal. As I exited the shuttle, I noticed a Polynesian couple crossing the street. My eyes didn't leave them. As we approached the automatic doors into the terminal, I saw their missionary tags.

I smiled. "It's great to see servants of the Lord getting ready to fly across the world to share the good news of Jesus Christ," I exclaimed. "Where are you headed?"

A big smile broke across the man's face while his wife glowed with friendliness. "We're going to New Guinea to serve as mission presidents." I glanced at his tag and saw the name President Fehoko.

"Can I help you with your bags, President Fehoko?" I asked.

Although they had many bags, both President Fehoko and his wife assured me they were fine. We spoke briefly before going our separate ways. The Fehokos went to check in their bags and I headed to Cafe Rio to grab a bite to eat.

After finishing my lunch, I headed toward the C gates for my flight. I spotted President Fehoko and his wife coming down the hallway from the opposite direction. Our paths merged once again as we turned toward the C gates. I began walking next to President Fehoko and initiated a conversation, "Where are you from, President?"

"We're from Tonga," he replied.

"Did you attend the mission presidents' training?" I asked.

"Yes. Yes," President Fehoko answered. "We just barely completed the training, and now we're flying off."

"Who provided the training and instruction?" I inquired.

"All of the apostles. They were all there. President Monson was the only one who didn't attend in person. However, he did speak to us via a live video conference."

"Wow! That must have been an amazing experience to be able to learn from those great men." I exclaimed.

It was now President Fehoko's turn to ask questions. "What's your name, brother?" he inquired.

"Cameron," I replied.

"Cameron, have you ever heard of the ceremony Rubbing Shoulders with the Brethren?"

Intrigued, I replied, "I haven't."

"As a part of the mission president training, there's a process that ensures each of the apostles physically rubs shoulders with each of the mission presidents."

President Fehoko must have seen the look of confusion on my face because he suddenly stopped walking and pulled me tightly next to his side, so we were shoulder-to-shoulder. "It was like this," he said.

President Fehoko began rubbing his shoulder vigorously against my shoulder. The initial impact of his shoulder pushed me to the side. He wrapped his arm around me and pulled me in tightly and again pressed his shoulder into mine. This time, I was more prepared for the impact, and I leaned into him to keep our shoulders together. He then vigorously rubbed his shoulder up and down and back and forth on my shoulder.

As quickly as the unique experience began, it ended, and he continued while we walked. "Just as I've rubbed shoulders with you, each of the apostles rubbed shoulders with me, as well as all of the other mission presidents who were in attendance. We were each touched by all of the apostles of the Lord Jesus Christ, rubbing shoulders with them before they sent us forth to preach the gospel to all the world."

"Did you feel their *mana*?" I asked.

President Fehoko replied, "Yes, yes. They filled me with great spiritual power. The apostles rubbed shoulders with the Lord Jesus Christ, and they were filled with Christ's love, power, and healing. The apostles then rubbed shoulders with each of the mission presidents to fill them with the same power. Every mission president is to rub shoulders with each missionary in their mission to fill them with Christ's power. The missionaries are to then carry the love, power, and healing of the Lord Jesus Christ to all the world."

The Spirit filled me as President Fehoko spoke. When he finished, I said, "When I saw you crossing the street to enter the airport earlier, I had the thought, 'There is a couple with tremendous *mana*.' I could feel the spiritual power you radiated. Thank you for rubbing shoulders with me."

As we concluded our discussion, we arrived at gate C9, which was my gate of departure. I again thanked President Fehoko and said goodbye as he continued on to gate C12.

I found a seat and pulled out my journal to record the experience. The Spirit affirmed in my mind that President Fehoko and I had been brought together by the hand of the Lord. I was in awe that God's guiding hand orchestrated someone from Tonga and someone from Idaho crossing paths twice in the Salt Lake City airport so I could be taught an important message. I felt the significance and importance of President Fehoko having been at that mission president conference to rub shoulders with the apostles to receive of Christ's love, power, strength, hope, and spirit. I felt the significance of President Fehoko sharing that power and spirit with me. By rubbing shoulders with President Fehoko, I had rubbed shoulders with all of the apostles and with the Lord Jesus Christ.

I felt a desire and responsibility to share the love and power I had received both with my family and with those I would be visiting in Moloka'i. I wanted to rub shoulders with them so they, too, could receive all that comes from rubbing shoulders with the prophets and apostles of the Lord Jesus Christ.

After a stop in Las Vegas and an uneventful six-hour flight from Las Vegas to Hawai'i, I arrived at the Honolulu airport. I walked to the small terminal for interisland flights. This relaxed, laid-back terminal was much more my style than the busy Honolulu airport terminals.

"You must be Cameron," the clerk said as I approached the counter.

I was surprised to be called by name, but since this plane only held eight passengers, it would be much easier to determine who each passenger was. After both me and my bag were weighed to ensure there wouldn't be too much weight on the small plane, I was directed outside to board. As I entered the plane, I glanced into the cockpit and was greeted by two friendly smiles. One of the pilots looked like he might still be attending high school. Trying not to show my surprise, I quickly smiled back and then headed to a window seat at the back of the plane.

The pilot's voice came over the intercom. After introducing

himself and welcoming us aboard, he good naturedly said, "For those of you who are wondering, yes, I've graduated from high school, and no, this isn't my first flight. And the gentleman sitting next to me is, in fact, the co-pilot and not my father." Laughter erupted throughout the plane as we prepared for takeoff.

Even though I've flown many, many times, I still get excited for takeoff. I looked eagerly out the window as we took flight. The beaches and buildings of Honolulu faded into the distance, overtaken by the deep blue of the Pacific Ocean. Thirty minutes later, Moloka'i's Kalaupapa Peninsula rose from the ocean. My mind raced as I pictured the leper colony that once graced the shores.

We landed at the Ho'olehua airport, and I made the short walk to the small terminal. As I entered, I spotted Manu. He was dressed in his usual attire of an Aloha shirt, cargo shorts, and flip-flops. He greeted me with a warm smile and loud *A-lo-ha*. He placed a flower lei around my neck, wrapped his arms around me, picked me up off the ground and said, "You look the same as when I last saw you twenty years ago. How is this possible?"

"Living the stress-free principles of Aloha you taught me has kept me young," I quipped with a smile. "It's so good to see you, Manu."

I waited for Manu to set me back on the ground before I pulled a flower lei from my bag and placed it around Manu's neck. "Aloha, Manu."

Manu nodded and replied, "*Mahalo*."

Manu gave me a firm slap on the back, and we began walking toward the parking lot. "I've already picked up our rental car. Are you ready to get to work?"

I smiled. "Sure. This is the kind of work I can get used to."

Manu laughed and replied, "Yes, it is. Yes, it is. When you love what you do, you never have to work a day in your life."

CHAPTER 5
SLOW DOWN

"I have a term I call Hawaiian Time. It is the ability to simply be still and listen to your heartbeat, to stop and observe a beautiful rainbow or to watch the dolphins dance with the ocean. I would make this a priority over getting to a destination on time—the ability of observation, appreciation, and relaxation. When I arrive at my destination, I'm much happier."

- Clifford Nae'ole

I followed Manu to the car, but tried to drink in as much of the scenery as I could. The rich smell of earth and plant life felt as though it pressed against my skin. All of it was in perfect harmony with one another. Even though I'd never been to Molokaʻi, it felt as though I belonged here. I kept my eyes scanning as we got in the car, still trying to take everything in.

"Naniwaiwai lives on the east end of the island in Hālawa Valley. It's about a thirty-mile drive from here," Manu said as we began.

I pulled out my map to see the path we would be driving. Molokaʻi is a thirty-eight mile long rectangle, spanning ten miles at its widest point north to south. The airport is near the center of the island, so we would be driving south toward the ocean and then east on the road along the south end of the island.

Manu made his way to the airport exit where a collection of signs covered a "T" in the road. One read, "Don't change Molokaʻi.

Let Moloka'i change you."

I read it out loud, and Manu replied, "This is a powerful message. The locals of Moloka'i have fought to protect the island from development and change to preserve their culture, ancient sites, and way of life. They have worked hard to protect the ancient way of Aloha. Moloka'i has the greatest proportion of those with Hawaiian lineage of any island, except Niihau. About half of the seven thousand people living on Moloka'i are of Hawaiian lineage."[15]

There was no traffic and we were immediately enveloped in the beauty of God's creations. As we drove peacefully, Manu said, "Just like on Lana'i, you will not find a single traffic light on the whole island."

"That's my kind of island," I replied.

"Yes, indeed. Moloka'i is called the "Friendly Island." The people are every bit as beautiful as their surroundings. So, Elder Taylor, how was your flight?" Manu asked.

"It was long, but that was good since it gave me time to ponder, sit in silence, and prepare myself to arrive on Moloka'i," I answered.

Manu continued with another question, "What did the 'āina [land] say to you when you set foot on the island?"

I pondered for a moment to gather my thoughts. "As I flew over Moloka'i, I recalled the feelings I had when my plane landed in Lana'i twenty years ago, and I stepped onto the island for the first time. I felt unity and harmony radiating from the 'āina. On the flight from Honolulu today, I studied the ocean, listened in stillness, and prepared myself to step foot on the sacred ground of Moloka'i. I asked the guardian angels of Moloka'i for permission to visit the island and partake of its beauty and knowledge. It's hard to describe what I felt as I stepped onto Moloka'i. The word that comes to mind is simplicity. Joy in being, instead of joy by doing. A feeling of seeking to enjoy, rather than seeking to possess. I feel that the *'āina* told me that Moloka'i is a place where life is simpler—where the rhythm and pace of life is more how life is supposed to be lived."

"I think you just described the message of Moloka'i perfectly, Elder Taylor."

I thanked Manu with "*Mahalo*" and continued, "You know you can call me Cameron, right? I'm not a missionary anymore."

Manu paused for a moment and then, with a big smile on his face replied, "Elder Taylor, you must remember that your trip here to Moloka'i is a mission. It's your second mission to Hawai'i, so I'll continue to call you Elder Taylor, if that's okay with you."

I was humbled by his response and grateful for the respect, honor, and love he showed me. Just being in Manu's presence made me a better person. I nodded my head, consenting to his desire to continue calling me Elder Taylor.

We passed homes nestled into the lush vegetation. I couldn't imagine a more pristine drive. The surroundings on Moloka'i made my heart rate slow. Even riding in a car felt slower than it did on the mainland.

"Elder Taylor, did you see the other signs that were posted as we left the airport?" Manu asked.

"No, Manu. That sign on letting Moloka'i change you jumped out at me and it occupied my thoughts, so I didn't pay attention to the other signs."

Manu continued, "One of the signs said, 'Aloha, slow down. This is Moloka'i.' This is a message for the visitors who don't have ears to hear the *'āina*, encouraging them to slow down. It's a message reminding visitors to respect and to not disrupt the culture and way of life on Moloka'i. There is a sign in one of my favorite places to eat on Moloka'i that says, 'If you're in a hurry, you're on the wrong island.'"

I grinned. Those words were certainly true. A few people leisurely walked along the road or waved from their front porch. Life definitely moved at a different pace here.

"I'm sure many visitors experience culture shock while on Moloka'i," I commented.

"Yes, Elder Taylor. I think you're right. Many from the mainland who have been raised in Western culture have been conditioned to a pace and hurry that's unhealthy and depleting. On the mainland, you will hear people speak about being 'burnt out' or 'not having enough time to get it all done.' The phrase 'getting it all done' isn't a phrase of Aloha or a phrase of the gospel of Jesus Christ. This is a false God of Western culture, legalism, and materialism. It results from a focus on things and tasks, instead of people and relationships. Knowledge is given through relationships and knowledge is for the purpose of improving relationships.

"Many people's calendars are full, but their lives are empty. Busyness destroys relationships. It substitutes shallow frenzy for deep friendship. It feeds the ego, but starves those who love us. It fills the calendar, but it fractures the family.[16]

"The principles of Aloha are simple, but isn't that the pattern for all truth? Truth is simple yet powerful. Simplicity is key to all of Hawaiian wisdom. When people learn the principles of Aloha, sometimes, they have a hard time believing it can be that simple."

"That reminds me of a quote by C.S. Lewis," I interjected. "'The real job of every moral teacher is to keep on bringing us back, time after time, to the old simple principles. Great moral teachers never introduce new moralities. Quacks and cranks do that.'"[17]

"Great quote, Elder Taylor. That's very true. Some from Western cultures look at the simple lives of those on Molokaʻi and think it's a step backward. Oh, how they are mistaken. A step to a simpler life isn't a step backward. It's a giant step toward a life of peace and joy.

"Jesus provides us with a perfect example. We must learn to emulate the life of Jesus Christ—a life without hurry or worry. Jesus went about doing good[18] but was never rushed or overscheduled. He was always present with those who were with Him. He didn't rush from person to person or from task to task. We can strive to emulate the Savior by living the principle of 'the one.' Jesus was able to focus on 'the one' He was with. He spent time with 'the one' as if that individual were His only friend. He was present. He didn't worry about the next person to heal or the next lesson to teach. He wasn't checking His texts or answering His phone. He wasn't planning the next day or thinking about a problem or deadline. His attention and love were on the one He was with and only the one.

"Many on the mainland are never present. They may be physically at the dinner table with their family, but they are somewhere else. Mentally, they may be at the office or checking Facebook or texts. For some people, technology keeps them from ever being fully present.

They are always somewhere else. We need to learn to be present as the Savior of the world was present."

I thought of my family. My wife and I had struggled to know how to keep technology from dominating our lives and the lives of our children. The words Manu spoke warmed my heart with truth.

"Elder Taylor," Manu's voice broke into my thoughts, "let me give you a piece of advice. When you're spending time with a child before bed, remember the principle of being present with the one and put aside all other tasks and thoughts. Put your phone away for the evening to avoid the distraction of texts and the temptation to read the most recent email or post. Give your child your full attention and love. Listen and speak while looking into their eyes. Be present with the one."

"There's power in the words you just shared," I said. "I know I must do better at disconnecting from work and technology so I can be fully present with my family. As you were speaking, the Spirit brought a story to my mind."

"I would love to hear it," Manu responded.

"My mom's current calling is preparing and printing the church program each week for sacrament meeting. One week, my mom was out of town and she asked me to complete the program in her absence. On Saturday evening, she texted me the final information for the program. I went to her home to enter the information into her computer and then began printing the programs. As I was waiting for the numerous pages to print, I began thinking about what to do next. I had the thought that once I finished this task, I could work on something more important. I was viewing the printing of the programs as an item to check off the to-do list.

"But the Spirit corrected me. He whispered to me, 'This is not just a task to complete. This is an opportunity to touch each member of your ward.' The Spirit brought this scripture to my mind, 'Whatever you do, work at it with all your heart, as working for the Lord.'[19]

"Although I had been physically printing the programs, I realized my heart hadn't been present in the task. After listening to the Spirit's correcting words, I decided to put my whole heart into the work. I began working for the Lord. I had the impression that as I touched each of the programs, I should fill each of them with the touch of the Lord Jesus Christ—with His touch of hope, His touch of faith, His touch of healing, His touch of love, His touch of light, and His touch of forgiveness.

"I prayed over the programs one by one as I folded them. I prayed that the peace, love, and hope of the Savior would fill the program. I prayed that as each person touched the program, they would feel the touch of the Master's hand and feel His touch of hope, love, and forgiveness.

"As I completed folding the programs, the Spirit brought another memory to my mind. A friend of mine in our ward had asked me for a priesthood blessing. During the blessing, I heard myself saying the words, 'You will be touched by the hands of the Lord Jesus Christ.' As I uttered those words, I felt two hands rest upon my own hands and on my friend's head. He was touched by the hands of His Savior. Tears streamed down both of our faces as we were filled with peace, love, and hope. Following the blessing, my friend stood from the chair and hugged me.

"He said, 'Thank you.' I held him tightly and said in return, 'I love you, brother.' 'I love you, too,' he replied.

"We each pulled tissues from the box on my desk. After we wiped the tears from our eyes, my friend asked, 'Did you feel the hands join the blessing?'

"I nodded my head as I said, 'Yes. We just experienced the fulfillment of the promise of the Lord found in the New Testament, 'For where two or three are gathered together in my name, there am I in the midst of them.'[20]

"After remembering this incident, I took the eighty folded programs, and I held them in my hands. I knelt and again prayed that the programs would be filled with the peace, hope, and love of the Lord Jesus Christ. I prayed that each member of our ward would be touched by the hands of the Savior as my friend was touched during his blessing. Tears poured down my cheeks as I prayed for each member of my ward. I could feel the love, peace, and hope of the Savior pour into the programs."

We drove in silence for a few moments, both of us pondering as the landscape grew more lush and full.

Manu broke the silence. "I was filled with the Spirit as you shared your experience. There is great love and power in the hands of the Master. Too often, we focus on the administration of tasks and checking off lists when we should focus instead on ministering to people and touching hearts. This is a powerful example of learning to be present with all your heart."

"I'm grateful the Spirit corrected me and taught me, so I didn't miss that opportunity to minister because I was focused on a task instead of focusing on Christ and people," I responded.

Manu continued, "Another principle that can help you slow down is to tarry a little longer. The book of Third Nephi in the Book of Mormon recounts the visit of Jesus Christ to the Americas following His resurrection. After teaching the people for a time, Jesus perceived that they were weak and were not able to understand all His words. Jesus instructed them to go home and prepare their minds, and He would return the next day.

"The people didn't want Jesus to leave, however, and they began to cry. Jesus cast His eyes upon the multitude and they 'did look steadfastly upon Him as if they would ask Him to tarry a little longer.'[21] Jesus didn't rush to His next appointment. Jesus tarried a little longer. He healed their sick. Jesus caused the blind to see, the lame to walk, and the deaf to hear. 'He took their little children, one by one, and blessed them, and prayed unto the Father for them. And when He had done this He wept.'[22] Jesus wasn't in a hurry. He would tarry a little longer.

"When you feel the rush and hurry so common in Western culture, pause for a moment and ask yourself the question, 'Should I tarry a little longer?' When you feel the desire to speed up, you most likely need to slow down."

The more we talked, the more I could feel the Spirit working within me. "Manu," I said, "your story from Third Nephi reminds me of the story President Monson shared in conference about his trip to Samoa. As the final hymn was announced, President Monson felt compelled to personally greet each of the children in attendance. The time was too short for such a privilege, though, so he ignored the impression. Before the benediction, however, he again felt a strong impression to shake the hand of each child.

"President Monson heeded the prompting and told the Samoan teacher that he wanted to shake the hand of each child. The teacher displayed a broad Samoan smile before relaying President Monson's intentions in Samoan to the children. The children beamed when they heard the translation. There was a special reason for their joy. When the children heard that an apostle of the Lord Jesus Christ would visit their tiny village, they began to pray that they would each have the opportunity to shake his hand. President Monson greeted and shook hands with each of the 247 children. Following the Savior's example, President Monson tarried a little longer, and as did the Savior when He blessed the children, President Monson wept."[23]

Manu nodded his head in agreement. "I love that story about President Monson. It's a great example of tarrying a little longer. We should each seek to follow the perfect example of the Savior of the world. The Savior's invitation to each of us is, 'Come unto me, all ye that labor and are heavy laden, and I will give you rest.'[24] The life of a Latter-day Saint should be a restful life. However, when you look at how many Latter-day Saints live, it would be described as anything but restful. Jesus didn't say, 'Come unto me, and I will give you more than you can possibly do.' Jesus didn't say, 'Come unto me, and I will give you stress.' He said, 'Come unto me, and I will give you rest.' If you wouldn't describe your life as a Latter-day Saint as restful, then there are doctrines of the gospel of Jesus Christ that you don't yet understand and live."

"So, Elder Taylor, what do you think?"

"I think there is much more I need to learn about rest," I answered.

Manu replied, "I've talked enough. You will learn what you need to know about rest and slowing down from God and the people and places of Moloka'i. Moloka'i has many lessons to teach us."

"Manu, listening to you teach as we drive surrounded by the beauty of the island has brought back great memories of our trips on Lana'i. I've missed living in Hawai'i and being with you."

Manu smiled, "I've missed you, too, Elder Taylor. We have a great adventure before us, and I'm excited to experience the adventure together."

I replied with a smile, "So far, the adventure is smoother than our adventures on Lana'i. I've not once hit my head on the window because of the rough road."

Manu laughed, "Well, don't get too comfortable, Elder Taylor. I'm sure you will hit your head a few times before our adventure is over."

CHAPTER 6
HĀLAWA VALLEY

"Nature helps us to see and understand God. To all His creations we owe an allegiance of service and a profound admiration... Love of nature is akin to the love of God; the two are inseparable."

- President Joseph F. Smith

Manu drove at a slow, steady pace. I happily soaked in the beauty of the island and Manu's spirit and teachings. I could hardly believe I was in Hawai'i again learning from Manu. We'd been traveling on a small, two-lane road with the ocean to our right and the mountains to our left for what seemed like only a few minutes, but in reality, we had been driving for over an hour.

The road turned north into the mountains and narrowed to the point that two cars traveling opposite directions could barely pass each other. The number and sharpness of turns increased. There were few other cars on the road, which was nice since the road eventually narrowed to one lane.

As we rounded one of the corners, a "Wow!" spontaneously escaped my lips. The road had climbed into the mountains so there was cliff on the ocean side of the road and we had a bird's-eye view of the beautiful bay below. The ocean was bright blue with crests of white waves flowing onto the sandy beach. Deep, beautiful green mountains surrounded and enclosed the bay.

Manu smiled at my reaction. "That's Hālawa Bay. It's a breathtaking sight every time you see it but even more so when you see it for the first time."

The narrow road continued to climb the mountain with sharp switchbacks. "We're just a few minutes from Naniwaiwai's home," Manu continued. "You will love Naniwaiwai. She radiates light, peace, love, and compassion. She will greet you with the traditional Hawaiian greeting called *honi*. In most of the islands, we now greet with a hug but on Moloka'i and Niihau, the Hawaiians continue to use the ancient *honi* greeting. The *honi* greeting is done by placing foreheads and noses together and inhaling at the same time.

"While the *honi* greeting may seem strange to some foreigners, it should not be foreign to any Jew or Christian. The Bible records the first *honi* greeting in the book of Genesis, 'The Lord God formed man of the dust of the ground and breathed into his nostrils the breath of life; and man became a living soul.'[25]

"God breathed nostril-to-nostril with man, sharing the breath of life with him. *Ha* is the sacred breath of creation—the breath of life. You will find *ha* all throughout the Hawaiian language, such as in *AloHA*, *MaHAlo*, *HAlawa*, and *HAwai'i*. *Ha* is a reminder that God is the sustaining force of life. *Ha* is a reminder that God is in us. *Ha* is a reminder of God's power, goodness, and generosity. *Ha* is the breath of life.

"The *honi* greeting is a reminder of the creation, that God is our creator, and a reminder that His breath gives us life. *Honi* is the joyful sharing of life and Aloha. When I greet someone with a *honi*, it causes me to slow down. My mind stops thinking about other things, and I become completely present with the person I'm with."

Feeling surprised, I interjected, "Why in my two years as I missionary in Hawaiʻi was I never greeted with a *honi*?"

Manu shrugged his shoulders. "The *honi* is sacred and has been used by Hawaiians for thousands of years. In more recent history, the *honi* has been protected from those who may not perform it with the proper respect and attitude. It's also a practice that some have simply forgotten. In the past decades, it has been exciting to see a resurgence of the *honi* throughout the islands."

We traveled slowly around the narrow, hairpin corners until the paved road came to an end. From there, we took a private dirt road into Hālawa Valley. We traveled for about a mile until we arrived at a small, old home surrounded by the same trees that filled the entire valley.

To the side of the home was a covered *lanai*, or porch. Manu removed his shoes and entered the *lanai*. I followed, removing my shoes as well. From the *lanai*, I could see a beautiful, well-kept *kalo* (taro) patch behind the home. *Kalo* is a root vegetable that's a staple of Hawaiian cuisine. The root is cooked and served like a potato or pounded into a paste called *poi*.

Manu and I walked to the edge of the *lanai* to admire the *kalo* patch. I heard the door from the home open and turned to see an older woman, who I assumed to be Naniwaiwai, stepping onto the *lanai*. She greeted Manu first, "Aloha, Manu."

Manu and Naniwaiwai approached each other and placed their

foreheads together and inhaled. Naniwaiwai's gaze then fell on me. "Aloha, Elder Taylor."

I approached Naniwaiwai and placed my forehead and nose against her and we inhaled.

As we pulled our heads apart, Naniwaiwai gently grabbed hold of my arms. She looked me in the eyes and said, "You bring with you great *mana*."

"Yes, Naniwaiwai, I do bring great *mana* with me, but it's not my own," I replied. The Spirit then prompted me to share with both her and Manu my experience rubbing shoulders with President Fehoko at the Salt Lake City airport earlier that day. After relating the complete experience to them, I said, "As I pondered on this experience, it was impressed upon my mind that I was to be an instrument in the hands of the Lord and His apostles to bring Christ's hope, love, power, and healing to Moloka'i."

Naniwaiwai came next to my side and asked, "May we rub shoulders with you as you did with President Fehoko, and like he did with the apostles?"

I had to bend down so my shoulder would be aligned with Naniwaiwai's, being careful not to press too hard against her 107-year-old frame. As we began rubbing shoulders, Naniwaiwai said, "I thought you said they rubbed shoulders vigorously and that President Fehoko almost knocked you over. You think I'm frail and old and you're frightened you will hurt me. While it's true that I was born one-hundred-seven years ago, I've grown stronger with each year."

Naniwaiwai leaned into me and bumped her shoulder into mine, causing me to take a step to keep my balance. I leaned back toward Naniwaiwai, and we vigorously rubbed our shoulders together. She seemed as strong as President Fehoko, who was four times her size.

When Naniwaiwai and I finished rubbing shoulders, I commented with surprise, "You're extremely strong."

Naniwaiwai smiled. "Strength is more about the size of one's heart than the size of one's body. True power is a function of the spirit."

Naniwaiwai was a woman with great *mana*. I was strengthened and lifted by her love and power as we shared breath in our greeting and as we rubbed shoulders. I was humbled and grateful to have this opportunity to be with her.

I worked to ground my heart and my spirit as Manu and I stood side-by-side, preparing to rub shoulders. When Manu and I completed the process, Naniwaiwai said, "It's a very, very rare occasion to have an apostle of the Lord Jesus Christ visit the island of Moloka'i, and today we've had fourteen apostles visit our island. I'll rub shoulders with each of my children and grandchildren so they, too, can say, 'I have rubbed shoulders with each of the Lord's twelve apostles.'"

Manu commented that he, too, would be sharing the experience and rubbing shoulders with those in his family. "Naniwaiwai, may I use your Bible?" Manu requested.

Naniwaiwai brought Manu her Bible and we sat down in the chairs on the *lanai*. Manu opened the book and began speaking, "The account of Christ's visit to the apostles following His resurrection was just brought to my mind."

Manu put his head down and began to read, "'Then…came Jesus and stood in the midst, and saith unto them, Peace be unto you. And when he had so said, he shewed unto them his hands and his side. Then were the disciples glad, when they saw the Lord. Then said Jesus to them again, Peace be unto you: as my Father hath sent me, even so send I you. And when he had said this, he breathed on them.'[26] John 20:22

"The account says that Jesus breathed on the apostles. Christ greeted the apostles with honi. He shared breath with them. Jesus is the breath of life. We share His life sustaining power and love during honi.

"In these scriptures, Jesus says, 'As the father sent me even so I send you.' So the rubbing of shoulders doesn't stop with rubbing shoulders with Jesus Christ. Jesus Christ rubs shoulders with the Father, so we, too, have rubbed shoulders with the Father. This scripture also shows the pattern of why the rubbing of shoulders is an important part of the mission president training and why it's important for each of the apostles to be at the training in person. Just as Heavenly Father sends Jesus Christ, Jesus Christ sends the apostles. The apostles say to the mission presidents, 'Even as Jesus sent us, so we send you.' The mission presidents say to their missionaries, 'Even as the apostles sent me, so I send you.' In this manner is the great commission of the Father accomplished to share the good news of Jesus Christ with all the world."

Naniwaiwai nodded her head multiple times in agreement. She paused and smiled before saying, "Now, it's time to ponder on these things as we eat. You two must be starving after a long day of travel. Please come inside. I have a feast prepared for you."

CHAPTER 7
DINNER WITH NANIWAIWAI

"Life is about connection—connections to other people, connection to the land, connections to God." [27]

- Reverend Abraham Akaka

We made our way to a dining table filled with food. I ran my fingers along the curves of a wooden spoon. After we sat down, Naniwaiwai offered a prayer in Hawaiian. Her words flowed and halted with the rhythm of the ocean breeze, rising and falling as though on the crest of a wave. The Spirit rushed over me as I listened to the beautiful sounds and rhythms of her prayer.

I found myself saying, "*Mahalo nui loa* [thank you very much]," at the completion of her prayer. Her prayer brought a spirit of peace, love and joy that couldn't go unacknowledged. Hearing Naniwaiwai pray brought these words to mind, "No one can conceive of the joy, which filled our souls at the time we heard [her] pray for us unto the Father."[28]

"I love hearing the Hawaiian language." My words seemed insufficient for how I truly felt.

"The Hawaiian language reveals truth and helps us to discover, understand, and live the principles of the gospel of Jesus Christ," Manu added. "The language connects us to God and truth. I believe the pure language to be spoken at the Lord's second coming[29] will sound much like what you just heard. A pure language is much more than words. A pure language is filled with *mana*, *ha*, and rhythm. The tone, the vibrations, the inflections, the spirit, the breathing, and the feeling are all a part of the language.

"The Hawaiian language is like music. Reading words in Hawaiian is like reading the lyrics to a song. To receive the full message and impact of a song, it must be heard. To receive the full impact and message of Hawaiian, it also must be heard. In the Book of Mormon, the words of Christ couldn't be written multiple times. I believe one of the reasons was because what Jesus shared was much more than words. It would be like trying to write down a song. Those recording the experience had no way of recording the music—the *mana*, the rhythm, the vibrations, the spirit, the breathing—that accompanied His words."

Naniwaiwai took my plate and filled it for me while Manu spoke. Steaming vegetables and fresh fruit created a colorful display. Everything looked and smelled delicious.

She then filled Manu's plate as she began to speak, "The Hawaiian language connects us to God and truth."

I picked up the wooden fork next to my plate to begin eating. Naniwaiwai asked, "Elder Taylor, have you ever eaten with a wooden fork?"

"No. I never have. The utensils are beautiful. Where did you get them?" I replied.

Naniwaiwai answered, "Everything you touch during this meal was made by hand from God-given creations. The table and chairs were hand crafted by a friend. The plates, forks, spoons, and cups were all hand-carved from naturally fallen wood on Moloka'i.

"Something magical happens when you use a bowl made by hand. Aloha and *mana* from the creator are stored in the bowl and transferred to the food, filling it with *mana* and Aloha. Food served from a bowl made with Aloha will not only fill the stomach but will fill the soul. You will be filled with passion, joy, light, and love. The food will breathe life into you. You can't eat from a Hawaiian *koa* bowl without connecting with the bowl's creator. You need that connection as much as you need oxygen." (The *koa* is a large Hawaiian tree which yields a fine, dark red wood.)

"We live in an age of plastics that are lighter and more durable than handcrafted bowls. However, there is no connection to others with a factory-produced bowl because artists haven't infused their *mana* and Aloha into it. The need for human connection is just as important today as it was a thousand years ago. The dollars to buy a plastic bowl may be less, but the cost of a plastic bowl is far too expensive for me since the costs of disconnection are great. Eating from a handmade bowl energizes life while eating from a mass-produced, plastic bowl weakens the body. Short term, the cost of the plastic bowl may appear to be less, but long term, it costs much, much more."

I was tempted to pull out my notebook and write down her wisdom. But I knew I must listen with my heart and receive with my spirit. I hoped by doing so, her words would be written on my heart where I could recall them later.

Naniwaiwai continued, "You need to connect with others every day to maintain your humanity. Our world is dying because many have forgotten how to connect with each other. [30] Too much of our world has become transactional, viewing people as objects, a means to an end, or as a mass market. Our world isn't to be a set of transactions but an ocean of relationships. Our world isn't a mass of people but a collection of individuals. Seek the item made for the one, not the item made for the masses."

"What do you mean by an ocean of relationships?" I asked.

"Some talk about how the ocean divides people," Naniwaiwai answered, "but Hawaiians have always seen the ocean as a connector. The eight seas between the islands join the islands together like a lei. Hawai'i isn't a group of islands separated by ocean but one whole of land and sea beautifully woven together by our divine Creator. The ocean unites us and is a part of our 'āina. The sea connects us with our neighbor islands and with the world. The more you connect with others, the stronger you are."

I could tell already that this dinner would be one never to be forgotten. I wanted to hear what Manu had to say on this topic, so I asked, "Manu, what are your thoughts?"

"Moloka'i is the center of Hawai'i, and Hawai'i is the center of the Pacific," Manu answered. "This isn't by chance. Hawai'i is a divine connector of people, places, and principles."

"Naniwaiwai, may I borrow your triple combination?" Manu asked.

Naniwaiwai pointed to an end table in her living room. Manu

rose from the table, returned with the scriptures, and began, "The prophesies and promises regarding the islands of the sea are numerous. The Book of Mormon says, 'Great are the promises of the Lord unto them who are upon the isles of the sea.'[31] Now listen carefully to this scripture from the Doctrine and Covenants, 'For behold, he shall stand upon the mount of Olivet, and upon the mighty ocean, even the great deep, and upon the islands of the sea, and upon the land of Zion.'[32] The books of Zenock and Zenos quoted in the Book of Mormon also contain promises and prophesy regarding the islands of the sea, which are similar in power and purpose to the promises and prophesies regarding Jerusalem and New Jerusalem. Hawaiʻi plays as important of a role in the history and salvation of mankind as Jerusalem and New Jerusalem. Aloha will change the world."

I listened and recalled my own trips to Jerusalem and New Jerusalem. There is a strong sense of divine history and future in each location. They are sacred and significant locations. I wasn't surprised to hear Manu speak of Hawaiʻi in such terms. There is no doubt that Hawaiʻi is a sacred place with great past and future significance in God's eternal plan.

Naniwaiwai spoke, "We live in a glorious time that was anticipated by all the prophets before us. The future has never looked so bright!"

"Elder Taylor, I can tell you're very eager to learn more about Hawaiʻi, but there will be plenty of time for that in the upcoming days. What I really want to learn right now is more about you and your family." We spent the remainder of the evening sharing about each other and our families, talking story, and eating until we were too tired to continue.

We helped Naniwaiwai put away the food and clean the kitchen. I was beginning to feel the effects of a very long day and was ready to sleep. As we finished cleaning, Naniwaiwai said, "As we conclude our day and as we begin this more important work, I feel it's important that we kneel and each pray vocally." Manu and I nodded our heads in agreement. "I'll begin. Manu, will you please pray next." Manu nodded. "Elder Taylor, will you please conclude our prayer." I nodded my consent. We knelt in a circle holding hands.

"We'll begin and complete our prayers with breathing. We'll inhale deeply together and say an extended '*ha*' as we exhale."

I peeked underneath my eyelids to see how Manu approached this breathing method. We began inhaling deeply in rhythm and exhaling with a whisper of "*haaaaaaaaaaaaaa.*" We repeated inhaling and exhaling for a few minutes until we stopped in unison. We sat in stillness and silence, until Naniwaiwai began to pray. Her voice cut through the warm air with such fervor and power. The softness of her voice made my ears eagerly strain for each syllable. We knelt in the stillness when she was done.

Then, Manu began to pray. The deep vibrations of his voice rumbled through the room, again sounding as though his words had a direct line to God. Stillness followed his prayer, too.

It was my turn now. Hoping to add to the deep sacredness that had filled the home, I spoke with sincerity of the desires and the concerns of my heart. My prayer was again followed with stillness and silence until we began to inhale deeply and exhaled with a whisper of "*haaaaaaaaaaaaaa.*"

Following the prayers, we embraced but no words were spoken. Naniwaiwai retired to her bedroom, Manu to the small guest room, and I to the living room couch.

CHAPTER 8

THE PROFOUND PRINCIPLES OF POI

"A peaceful heart leads to a healthy body."

- Proverbs 14:30, NLT

I awoke to the crowing of roosters. I looked at the clock. It was 6:07 a.m. I was still adjusting to Hawaiian time and my body was definitely not ready to wake up yet. However, with a little internal coaxing, I won the battle with the blanket and got ready for the day.

As I went out onto the *lanai*, I saw Naniwaiwai in her backyard next to her *kalo* fields using a traditional *papa kuʻi ʻai* (*kalo* pounding boards) and *kuʻi ʻai pōhaku* (*poi* pounder) to make *poi*.

She called to me, "Elder Taylor, come, come."

I went to her side and watched as she pounded the *kalo*. "Have you ever made *poi*?" Naniwaiwai asked.

"I've not, but I would like to," I answered.

"*Poi* is made from the root of the *kalo* plant. ʻ*Ohā* is the word for the ancient *kalo* root from which all *kalo* has sprung. The *kalo* plant was the staple of life in ancient Hawai'i and was the main source of food and medicine. The word 'ohana [family] comes from the highly reverenced word 'ohā—signifying that all people come from the same root—God. The making of poi is sacred. It's an important process of connecting with 'oha—connecting with Christ and our ancestors."

I took a seat and watched and listened. The rhythmic movements of her hands never stopped as she spoke.

"Our world is becoming more and more disconnected. The more distant we are from our food source, the more disconnection we create. Ancient Moloka'i was a land of prosperity and independence. This valley was the thriving community of thousands for many, many generations. The farms and fish ponds produced in great abundance. Today, there are only a few families left in Hālawa Valley and ninety-five percent of what's consumed on Moloka'i is imported. With the importation of food and resources, Moloka'i has lost some of its connection to 'ohā and much of its independence. If the barges stopped coming to Moloka'i, there would be widespread starvation in three weeks.

"This problem isn't unique to Moloka'i. The same trend has occurred in the mainland with fewer and fewer people growing and harvesting their own food. Their food comes from further and further distances. This food may fill the belly, but it robs the soul.

"Naniwaiwai means beautiful abundance. It was a name given me to honor this valley and this island. Moloka'i is a land of beautiful abundance. To preserve and perpetuate this beautiful abundance, we must grow our own kalo and pound our own poi. The making of poi helps keep us connected to our 'ohana and our God."

I was filled with admiration as I watched Naniwaiwai pound and work the *kalo*. The Spirit and knowledge of Moloka'i flowed with her faith, strength, and wisdom. I had a hard time believing she was a-hundred-and-seven years old.

This was only a thought, but it was as if Naniwaiwai could read my mind. "There are many benefits of Aloha and one of those is health and longevity," she said. "The life expectancy in the mainland is around seventy-eight years young. If they added more Aloha to their way of life, I believe that average could easily exceed one hundred years."

My admiration increased further as I witnessed Naniwaiwai use the gift of discernment to perceive my thoughts.

"Well, Elder Taylor, it's your turn to make some *poi*. Please retrieve some *kalo* from the *imu* (underground oven)," Naniwaiwai said as she pointed. I hadn't seen one in years but so many good and delicious memories started with an *imu*. While modern ovens are convenient, they can't beat the *imu*.

I retrieved the *kalo* and sat on the ground opposite of Naniwaiwai with the *poi* board between us. I placed the *kalo* onto the board and began to crush it with the *poi* pounder. I could feel the fibers of the *kalo* flexing and grinding under my hand. There was something satisfying about making food this way as it had been done for centuries.

"Elder Taylor, making *poi* in Hālawa Valley will connect you with the people of this place," Naniwaiwai said. "My *'ohana* has lived in this valley for thousands of years. Our genealogy has been preserved and passed down for fifty generations. To assist you in connecting with our ʻohana, I'll chant our family genealogy as we work."

The names came softly at first but as she moved on, the pitch of her voice rose and fell. The love of her family filled the air and permeated into our work.

As she chanted, tears rolled down my cheeks. I felt the presence of her ʻohana. We were surrounded by angels. I continued to smash the kalo onto the board, but I was doing much more than making poi. I was connecting with the ʻoha of Hālawa Valley.

Naniwaiwai finished her chant, and we worked in silence for a few minutes. "My mother always told me the main ingredient in poi is Aloha. Poi becomes filled with the mana of its maker. If you're bitter and angry when you cook, your food will be filled with bitterness and anger. If you're full of laughter and joy as you cook, your food will be filled with joy and laughter. The making of poi is sacred. Only those who are pono—those who are in harmony with God—are allowed to make it."

We spent the next few minutes talking story, laughing, singing, and smiling as we completed making the poi and gathering it into a large wooden bowl. She told me about her children and grandchildren. I told her about each of my children and the long list of activities they were expecting when they finally get to come to Hawaiʻi. I couldn't help but talk about my wife, too. Though I knew I was here with a great purpose, leaving for even a short time made me ache a little.

As we walked toward Naniwaiwai's home, she said, "Now, this is food that will feed the body and the soul. There is a Hawaiian saying, 'Ono kāhi ʻao lūʻau me ke Aloha pū,' which means that even the simplest food is delicious when made with love."

As we entered the home, we found Manu in the living room, studying the scriptures.

Manu greeted me, "Aloha, I see you made *poi* with Naniwaiwai. It's a life-changing experience, yes?"

I nodded my head in agreement, knowing I would never view the world the same. My eyes had been opened a little further.

Naniwaiwai motioned for Manu to come to the table. "Come eat. Come eat."

I placed the bowl of *poi* at the center of the table, which she surrounded with a variety of fruits, vegetables, and nuts. She invited Manu to pray and open the bowl of *poi*.

I wasn't sure what she meant by opening the bowl of *poi* since the bowl had no covering.

Following the prayer, Manu began, "It's customary before we begin eating from a new bowl of *poi* to evaluate relationships. It's a reminder to have a forgiving spirit. *Poi* can keep without refrigeration, so it's common to keep a large bowl of *poi* at the center of the table for several days to be eaten with meals. As the *poi* sits, it begins to develop a sour crust around the edges. The sour crust of the *poi* bowl is a reminder that an unforgiving spirit will develop into a sour crust.

"Just as a new bowl of *poi* is free from a sour crust, so should we be free of grudges and conflict. If there happens to be a conflict or incident that needs to be resolved, a *hoʻoponopono* session can be held for reconciliation and forgiveness to ensure an atmosphere of unity and harmony. The tradition of forgiveness when opening a new bowl of *poi* is a way of keeping our relationships sweet and free of crust."

"Elder Taylor, you experienced the sacred nature of *kalo* and *poi* this morning and witnessed how it connects us with Christ and our ancestors. Because it's sacred, there should be harmony, peace, and respect when a bowl of *poi* is opened. There are to be no arguments or fighting. Eating around the *poi* bowl is a time for pleasant socializing."

Manu placed two fingers into the center of the bowl and twisted the *poi* onto his fingers. As he held the *poi* on his fingers, he said, "It's our family tradition to open a new bowl of *poi* by saying, "'*Lawe i ka manawa e'ai ai i ka poi,*' which means, 'Take time to eat *poi.*'"

Naniwaiwai smiled at Manu and said, "*Mahalo.*"

Manu placed his fingers into his mouth and ate the *poi* from his fingers. "*Ono* [delicious]," Manu exclaimed.

I took a banana, a mango, and some macadamia nuts. I placed two fingers on the side of the *poi* bowl nearest to me somewhat reluctant but willing to try.

Manu gently corrected, "It's custom to eat from the center of the bowl."

I moved my fingers to the center of the bowl and twisted the *poi* onto my fingers. Manu then asked me a question, "Elder Taylor, *pehea kou piko?*"

I gave Manu a puzzled look. Even though I knew the individual words he had just spoken, this Hawaiian phrase wasn't one I was familiar with and seemed a little strange. "Manu, did you just ask me, 'How is your belly button?'"

Chuckling, Manu replied, "Yes. That would be one translation. A better translation would be 'How is your navel?' or 'How is your center?' *Pehea kou piko?* was a very common greeting among our ancestors. *Piko* is the Hawaiian word for navel or center. Eating from the center of the bowl is a reminder to keep your life centered on God. If you're centered on God, your body and spirit will operate in faith, harmony, peace, love, and joy. If your center moves away from God, you lose balance and harmony and experience fear, discord, stress, anger, sickness, and dysfunction.

"*Piko* is also the word for the umbilical cord that once connected you to your mother and is symbolic of your connection to your ancestors and descendants. So '*pehea kou piko?*' also means, 'how is your connection to family?'

"Genealogy is a part of all Hawaiian life. Genealogy creates connection, and connection creates power. A line connects you to your ancestors and a line connects you to your posterity. *Piko* is symbolic of that connecting line. When someone has done something that disrupts the family chain, we say that person is out of line or out of center. You're the center between your ancestors and your descendants. You want to stay in line by living in a way that honors the generations before you and perpetuates Aloha for the generations to follow. When you stand in line—when you're centered—you receive great *mana* from your ancestors who came before you and your posterity who will come after you.

"The sealing rooms in the temple illustrate this concept powerfully. In a sealing room, there are two mirrors facing each other on opposite walls. When you stand in the center of a sealing room and look into one of the mirrors, you see your reflection dozens of times. This represents your ancestors. As you turn one-hundred-and-eighty degrees to look into the other mirror, you again see your reflection dozens of times. This represents your posterity. When you stand in the center, all the reflections stand with you. If you step out of line with the mirrors, the reflections disappear. When you step out of line, you break the connection. Eating from the center of the *poi* bowl is a reminder to stay centered, to keep the lines of genealogy connected and unbroken.

"I mentioned yesterday that no Christian should be surprised by the sharing of breath. Similarly, no Latter-day Saint should be surprised to find discussions about the navel in Hawaiian culture. The scriptures and the temple ceremonies are filled with references to the navel. Probably the most well-known verse is in Doctrine and Covenants section 89, 'And all saints who remember to keep and do these sayings… shall receive health in their navel and marrow to their bones.'[33] The book of Job declares, 'Force is in the navel of his belly.'[34]

"*Na'au* is a Hawaiian concept of a guiding force in the gut. It's often described in English as your gut-reaction, intuition, or instincts. Although *na'au* is often translated into English as gut, I think a better translation would be the scriptural term bowels. Our bowels are a receptacle of our moral nature—our character.

Manu continued, "For many generations, our *kūpuna* have shared a story about our bowl of light. They teach that at birth, each child is a bowl of perfect light. If the child tends this light, the light will grow in strength and the child can do all things—swim with the shark, fly with the birds, and know and understand all things. If, however, the child becomes envious or jealous, the child drops a stone into the bowl of light and some of the light dissipates. Since the light and the stone cannot hold the same space, if the child continues to put stones in the bowl of light, the light will eventually be extinguished, and the child will become a stone. A stone doesn't grow, nor does it move. If, at any time, the child tires of being a stone, all he needs to do is turn the bowl upside down and the stones will fall away and the light will grow once more.[35]

"Another greeting common among our ancestors was *ʻpehea ka lā?* This greeting is a reference to your bowl of light and is a thoughtful and caring question regarding how you're tending your light. *ʻPehea ka lā?* would literally translate to 'How is the sun?' but as you know, Hawaiian is a very symbolic and metaphorical language with deep imagery and meaning that's often tied to a story. One who didn't know the bowl of light story may not understand the greeting *ʻpehea ka lā?* However, the bowl of light story was a well-known and integral part of life and language among our ancestors.

"The Lord often associated feelings and character with His *naʻau*. He said, 'Behold, my bowels are filled with compassion toward you. Have ye any that are sick among you? Bring them hither. Have ye any that are lame, or blind, or halt, or maimed, or leprous, or that are withered, or that are deaf, or that are afflicted in any manner? Bring them hither and I will heal them, for I have compassion upon you; my bowels are filled with mercy.'[36]

"The Lord's bowels, His bowl of light, His *naʻau*, is filled with compassion and mercy. The greeting of *ʻpehea kou piko?* and *ʻpehea ka lā?* could also be interpreted 'How are your bowels?' and 'What are your bowels filled with?'

"The bowels are a receptacle of our thoughts, acts, and virtue. Our bowels should be filled with love, truth, compassion, mercy, generosity, and goodness. Our bowels should be a bowl of light.

"When we lie, cheat, are unkind or greedy, we often experience our stomach being tied into knots because we've violated a principle of truth and virtue. We have a rock in our bowl of light, which needs to be removed.

"Elder Taylor, next time you do initiatory work in the temple, listen carefully to the references to your bowels. The next time you're in a sealing room of the temple, take a moment to stand in the center of the room and look into the mirrors to connect with your ancestors and descendants. The next time you do an endowment session, listen carefully to the references to your navel. The Lord has been asking *'pehea kou piko?'* and *'pehea ka lā?'* in the temples since the days of Adam."

CHAPTER 9
HĀLAWA BAY

"If we will humbly present ourselves before the Lord and ask Him to teach us, He will show us how to increase our access to His power." [37]

- President Russell M. Nelson

We finished breakfast and cleaned the kitchen. The bowl of *poi* remained at the center of the table.

"Manu, I think you should take Elder Taylor down to Hālawa Bay this morning and share with him the stories of our ancestors coming to Molokaʻi," Naniwaiwai said.

Manu nodded his head in agreement. "You ready to go, Elder Taylor?"

"Of course." Hālawa Bay wasn't far from the house and stretching my legs sounded good after spending a day traveling.

"Okay, let's go. Naniwaiwai, will you be joining us?"

"I'll always be with you, but my physical body will remain here," Naniwaiwai said with a smile.

I watched Manu to see how far our walk would be, whether I would need my sandals or shoes. I was relieved to see that it was sandals. The anticipation of sand between my toes made me that much more eager.

It was a magnificent morning. The trees formed a graceful green canopy above us, creating patterns of light and shade on the path. The peaceful sound of a light breeze flowed through the leaves. The birds chirped as they flew from tree to tree. Red and yellow flowers were intermittently sprinkled throughout the lush, green landscape, making all the green seem brighter and deeper. I took a deep breath, expanding my lungs as though I could breathe it all in.

As we walked down the red dirt road, Manu shared, "There are many theories and opinions on when and how the Hawaiian Islands were populated. The theories and opinions of scholars vary greatly and are continually changing. Much of the current thinking is that the first people came to Hawai'i from the West around 400 AD. While it may be true that people came to Hawai'i around 400 AD from the West, I don't believe these were the first people.

"Based on oral traditions from Moloka'i and the other Pacific islands, I believe Moloka'i was populated before the coming of Christ by people from the Americas. Many chants and stories talk of voyagers coming to Moloka'i from the East. There are many family genealogies that extend before the coming of Christ.

"These ancient Hawaiian songs and chants that have been repeated for many centuries teach that Moloka'i is the source from which all the islands were inhabited. Elder Taylor, have you been to the Bishop Museum in Honolulu?"

"I haven't."

"I'll definitely have to take you on one of your next trips to Hawai'i. It's a magical place. They have the world's largest collection of

Hawaiian artifacts. In a television documentary made by the Bishop Museum, they pinpointed Hālawa as first settlement of Hawai'i."

Manu definitely had my attention. Hawaiian history fascinates me.

"An archaeological survey of Hālawa Valley found it to be the oldest archaeological site on Moloka'i. This survey confirmed that Hālawa Valley was once a thriving community of thousands who developed innovative and advanced agricultural systems, which included at least seven hundred irrigated taro fields.[38] They also developed advanced aquafarming and fish management systems. There are seventy-three fishponds along a forty-mile stretch of Moloka'i's south shore. The ancient Hawaiians were brilliant farmers of the land and the sea.

"The first Christian missionaries arrived in Hawai'i in 1820. The Hawaiians who assisted in translating the Bible into Hawaiian were inspired by the Bible's similarity to their ancient traditions. The Old Testament stories were very similar to Hawaiian stories that had been passed down for many generations. These similar stories included the story of creation, Adam and Eve and the Garden of Eden, Noah, Abraham, the tower of Babel, Jonah, and Moses. The story of Joseph who was sold into Egypt is the Hawaiian story of Waikelenuiaiku. The Old Testament and Hawaiian stories are so similar that the only rational explanation is that our ancestors brought these stories with them to Hawai'i."

Ahead of me, I could see the beach and ocean. Pointing to a small park and pavilion near the beach, Manu said, "Let's go here for a minute. I have a few quotes to share with you."

We sat down at one of the picnic tables. Manu retrieved a small book from his pocket and began flipping through its pages. His fingers stopped on a page and he began reading, "The first Mormon missionaries arrived in Hawaiʻi in 1850. George Q. Cannon was one of the first LDS missionaries to Hawaiʻi. While Elder Cannon was at Lahaina, on the island of Maui, he received knowledge directly from the Lord that the Hawaiians were of the house of Israel. From this time on, Elder Cannon and his associates began to teach that the Hawaiian people were a branch of the house of Israel."[39]

Manu continued, "While speaking to a group of Hawaiian saints in Laie, Elder Matthew Cowley said, 'Brothers and sisters, you are God's children—you are Israel. You have in your veins the blood of Nephi.'[40]

"In the 1962 general conference, Elder Mark E. Petersen said, 'The Polynesian Saints are characterized by a tremendous faith. Why do they have this great faith? It is because these people are of the blood of Israel… God is now awakening them to their great destiny. As Latter-day Saints, we have always believed that the Polynesians are descendants of Lehi and blood relatives of the American Indians, despite the contrary theories of other men.'[41]

"During the dedicatory prayer at the Laie Hawaiʻi Temple, President Heber J. Grant said, 'We thank Thee that thousands and tens of thousands of the descendants of Lehi, in this favored land, have come to a knowledge of the gospel.'[42]

Manu paused and then emphatically stated, "There is no doubt in my mind that Hawaiians have the blood of Israel running through their veins."

I nodded my head and said, "I remember several general authorities came to speak to the missionaries. They told us that the people of Hawai'i are of the house of Israel—that they are Christ's other sheep and will hear and recognize His voice. I witnessed this firsthand as a missionary as I saw many Hawaiians unite with the saints as they heard the good news of Jesus Christ and His restored church and followed the Good Shepherd."

The importance of the connection between the Hawaiians and the House of Israel sank deep into my heart. The power and strength of Manu's words penetrated my entire body.

"Should we head over to the bay now, Elder Taylor?"

I nodded, and we arose from the table and made the short walk from the pavilion to the bay. The Hālawa Stream runs from the mountains of Hālawa Valley into the bay. The stream cuts a path through the beach and into the ocean. We found a shallow spot in the stream to wade across to the beach. In the middle of the stream, the cool, refreshing water came to my thighs.

Manu and I were the only two people on the beach. The sand was untouched. A small thrill coursed through me at being the first visitors of the day. The view of Hālawa Bay from the winding mountain road the day before was one of the most spectacular sights I had ever seen. As I stood on the beach, the history and Aloha that radiated from the *'āina* was sacred. I felt as if I were at the beginning of time witnessing the creation. There was a feeling of peace, love, and wonder. I was sure this was how life was meant to feel.

We stood in silence, absorbing the beauty of the bay. Ocean waves rolled in breaking on the shore in a peaceful rhythm. I turned and looked at the crystal-clear water of Hālawa Stream. My eyes followed the stream all the way from the beach to the luscious, dark green valley and the majestic mountains. I could see waterfalls dotting the distant landscape. As my eyes continued upward, they connected with an exquisite, blue sky. We were surrounded by mountains, waterfalls, valleys, rivers, streams, a beach, and the ocean—all in a single location.

Manu sat on the sand. I followed and sat by his side. "The stories of the first settlers coming from the East have been passed down for many, many generations," Manu said.

"There is no ancient reference to the first settlers coming from the West. Our chants talk of God leading a people on a long journey from the East and landing at this very place." Manu stretched his arms wide, his hands open as if he were holding Hālawa Bay.

"The Hawaiians are among those spoken of in 1 Nephi 22:4, 'And behold, there are many who are already lost from the knowledge of those who are at Jerusalem. Yea, the more part of all the tribes have been led away; and they are scattered to and fro upon the isles of the sea.'

"Christ told the Jews[43] and the Nephites[44] that he was going to visit his other sheep that weren't in Jerusalem or America. The Hawaiians are a part of the other sheep Jesus spoke of. He visited Hawai'i following His resurrection, and a Zion society was established in Hawai'i similar to those societies established in Israel and in America. Zion societies were established within all of the tribes of Israel that were scattered throughout the earth.

"The New Testament records Christ's earthly ministry in Israel.

Christ called twelve apostles, established His Church and started a Zion society where the people had all things in common. The attempt at Zion in Israel didn't last very long. All the apostles were murdered before 100 AD. Likewise, the Book of Mormon records Christ's visit to the Americas following His resurrection and the establishment of a Zion society there. The Zion society in America fared much better than the Zion society in Israel and it lasted about two hundred years. However, by the end of the Book of Mormon, around 400 AD, any resemblance to Zion had vanished."

Manu continued, "Eventually, there was an apostasy from Zion in all locations throughout the world. Some only lasted a few years, while others lasted for hundreds of years. I believe that the Zion established in Hawaiʻi was the longest-lasting Zion society, and that more of the principles of Zion have survived in Hawaiʻi than in any other location. The principles of Aloha and the principles of Zion are the same. As a people, we're seeking for Zion. Many have tried to establish Zion and failed. I believe a key to creating Zion is found in the lives of the ancient Hawaiians. Aloha is needed to prepare a Zion people to be ready to greet and embrace the Savior and Redeemer of the world at His second coming.

"Throughout Hawaiʻi, there are oral traditions of sacred records that are preserved in mountain caves, which contain the words of the prophets of Hawaiʻi as well as Christ's visit to the islands following His resurrection. In the Book of Mormon, Christ confirms this is true, saying, 'For behold, I shall speak unto the Jews and they shall write it [Bible]; and I shall also speak unto the Nephites and they shall write it [Book of Mormon]; and I shall also speak unto the other tribes of the house of Israel, which I have led away, and they shall write it … For I command all men, both in the east and in the west, and in the north, and in the south, and in the islands of the sea [Book of Aloha], that they shall write the words which I speak unto them.'⁴⁵

"Elder Taylor, I believe one of the reasons a Zion society was able to endure for so long in Hawai'i was the fact that Hawai'i was isolated from outsiders who would seek to conquer her and destroy her culture. Hawai'i is the most secluded land on the planet. California is the closest land mass at 2,400 miles away. Japan is the closest land to the west and is 3,900 miles away.

"Unfortunately, Zion eventually came to an end even in Hawai'i when the islands were conquered by warriors from Tahiti between 1200 and 1300 AD. According to an ancient Hawaiian chant, Pa'ao gathered thousands of warriors to travel to Hawai'i to conquer the islands. 'The people on Lana'i were the first to see them approaching. They said the red *malo* [clothes] of the invaders could be seen from horizon to horizon, making the sea itself take on a red hue. Soon, the sea did turn red with the blood of our people, as thousands were slaughtered and enslaved.'⁴⁶ Some were able to escape Lana'i by boat and headed for the island of Kaua'i for safety. The natives knew you had to be very skilled and experienced with the tides of Kaua'i to get ashore safely. On their way to Kaua'i, they stopped at Moloka'i to warn the people of the attacking Tahitians.

"The people of Moloka'i gathered along the southern coastline and stood in silence. When the Tahitian war canoes appeared on the ocean horizon, the people began to chant. As the Tahitians came closer and closer, their chanting became louder and louder. A mighty chanting roar met the Tahitians as they approached the beach. The Tahitians stood up in their canoes and began hurling spears. All the spears fell short, appearing to hit an unseen wall. The Tahitians brought their canoes to shore and rushed up the beach to attack, but were met by the same impenetrable, invisible wall. They found themselves choking and gasping for air. Some were picked up by an invisible force and flung back into the ocean. The people of Moloka'i continued to stand and pray in unison. The Tahitians became afraid of the island and its people. They ran to their canoes and fled.

"The Tahitian warriors were giants compared to the ancient Hawaiians. The average Tahitian warrior was around seven feet tall while the average ancient Hawaiian was less than five feet tall."

A low whistle escaped my lips. I could almost see the scene as giants charged up the beach. It was an honor to be on the beach where such an act of faith took place.

"While the people of Moloka'i were small in stature, they were spiritual giants. The people of Moloka'i used their *mana* (spiritual power) and *pule* (prayer) to protect their *'ohana* (family) and island. Moloka'i was the only Hawaiian island not conquered by the Tahitians. The Tahitians easily conquered the other islands as the people were fisherman and farmers, not warriors. The people of Hawai'i lived in peace and harmony and had no need for an army or weapons of war. In a second attempt to conquer the island of Moloka'i, the Tahitians returned with even more warriors and their strongest spiritual leaders. Despite this, the Tahitians were unable to defeat the people of Moloka'i. Following these battles, the Tahitians called Moloka'i *Pule O'o*, meaning Island of Powerful Prayer.

"The power of my ancestors didn't come by the sword or the spear, but by faith in the Lord Jesus Christ. The people of Moloka'i utilized the powerful promise found in the Doctrine and Covenants, 'The weak shall confound the wise, and the little one become a strong nation, and two shall put their tens of thousands to flight.'[47] Elder Taylor, my heritage has taught me that two saints with faith in the Lord Jesus Christ can cause an army of tens of thousands to flee.

"Moloka'i remained independent as Pa'ao and the Tahitians became the rulers of the other Hawaiian islands. They called themselves *ali'i* (the rulers or chiefs) and war was their way of life. They were always fighting—brother fought brother, father fought son.[48] The Tahitians battled for control of the islands through slaughter and force and Hawai'i would never be the same. Peace was replaced with war. Work was replaced with plunder. Community was replaced with a ruling class and slavery. The way of Aloha was replaced with a strict law called *kapu*. Violators of the *kapu* were executed or used as human sacrifices. 'What most people today regard as the religious system of the old Hawaiian people was not their true religion—it was a foreign religion introduced by the invader Pa'ao... The Hawaiian people endured much suffering and bondage under this new religious system.'[49]

"Even though Moloka'i wasn't immediately conquered by Pa'ao, they eventually fell victim to the tyranny and oppression of the ruling class and the *kapu* system that was established throughout Hawai'i. However, Aloha never died. It lived on in the hearts of the people.

"Elder Taylor, be careful not to mix the practices and principles of *kapu* with the principles and practices of Aloha. The *ali'i* from Tahiti were the ones to institute human sacrifice and many other apostate practices. The *ali'i* desecrated many Hawaiian *heiau* (temples) by using them for idol worship and human sacrifice. The *heiau* before 1200 AD had no tiki idols and no human sacrifices.

"The *ali'i* sought power and control with the apostate practices of *kapu*. Despite this horrific tyranny and abuse, the Hawaiians retained Aloha in their hearts as they looked forward to a day when peace would return to the island and they would be freed from the cruel, oppressive *kapu* system with its false gods and idols. In ancient Hawai'i, there were no kings or rulers and there was no system of strict laws and rules. They were governed by *'ohana* and Aloha.

"On October 3, 1819, six months after the death of Kamehameha the Great, the bondage of the *kapu* system was broken. Ka'ahumanu and Ke'opuolani, two brave women who were wives of Kamehameha the Great openly broke the *kapu* by eating together with the new king, Liholiho (Kamehameha II), at a formal state occasion. This was an undeniable public act of defiance. It sent an unmistakable message: the *kapu* system was no longer honored by the king and the highest *ali'i* in the land.

"These three highest *ali'i* were supported by Kamehameha's prime minister, Kalanimoku, and also the highest *kahuna* in the land, Hewahewa, who was a direct descendant of Pa'ao. Hewahewa was the first to set flame to false idols saying, 'I knew the wooden images of deities, carved by our own hands, could not supply our wants, but worshipped them because it was a custom of our fathers… My thought has always been, there is one only great God, dwelling in the heavens.'[50]

"There were many prophecies both during the time of *kapu* and following its demise that the one true God of peace worshipped before the coming of Pa'ao and the *kapu* system would return to Hawai'i. Six months after the *kapu* system was abolished, the first Christian missionary arrived, fulfilling these prophesies. Many recognized Jesus Christ as the God of light and peace they had worshiped and followed before *kapu*. A census taken in 1853 showed that ninety-six percent of Hawaiians claimed membership in a Christian church.[51] Hawai'i was once again one of the greatest Christian nations on the earth."

Manu stopped talking for a time and we sat on the beach in silence. Even though no words were spoken, I could hear the *'āina* and the Spirit continue to teach me as we sat in this sacred place.

After a time, Manu broke the silence with a question, "What are your thoughts, Elder Taylor?"

"I was filled with power as you shared the history of this place, Manu. The Spirit bore witness to me that what you were sharing was true. I'm excited to share the story of the mighty prayer of the people of Moloka'i. Today our families are being attacked by the armies of Satan. Fathers, mothers, and children need to pray with faith and power as did the people of Moloka'i. Satan will be unable to penetrate their walls of faith and their prayers will throw Satan from their presence. He will flee from before them.

"These homes will be called *Hale Pule O'o* (House of Mighty Prayer), and the power and protection of heaven will fill their hearts and homes. Satan's attempts to destroy their souls will fail. These mighty men and women of God will not fear Satan and his armies. Satan and his armies will fear them, for they will know if they engage them in battle, they will be crushed by their shields of faith and cut with their swords of truth."

The Spirit brought a scripture into my mind and I recited it to Manu. "'Let us be strong like unto Moses; for he truly spake unto the waters of the Red Sea and they divided hither and thither.'[52] 'Let us be strong like the people of Moloka'i; for they spake unto the God of heaven and their enemies were tossed into the sea.'"

Manu nodded his head in agreement and turned to me with a smile and asked, "Can you see why the Lord has brought you to this place?"

I nodded my head.

Manu continued, "As you spoke, the Spirit brought a quote to my mind."

Manu pulled out his book of notes and after searching through several pages began speaking, "President Russell M. Nelson has urged us to pay the price to obtain spiritual power. He said, 'I fear that there are too many priesthood bearers who have done little or nothing to develop their ability to access the powers of heaven… I urgently plead with each one of us to live up to our privileges as bearers of the priesthood. In a coming day, only those men who have taken their priesthood seriously, by diligently seeking to be taught by the Lord Himself, will be able to bless, guide, protect, strengthen, and heal others. Only a man who has paid the price for priesthood power will be able to bring miracles to those he loves and keep his marriage and family safe, now and throughout eternity.'"[53]

President Nelson's words penetrated my soul. I felt a *kuleana* rest on my shoulders to help the saints pay the price to build their faith and power.

CHAPTER 10
ʻAUMĀKUA

"The spirits are with you, guiding you, all the time."

- Kahuna Keola Sequeira

I was still deep in my own thoughts when Manu rose to his feet. We waded across the stream in silence. As we traveled back to Hālawa Valley, Manu said, "I think there is great wisdom in Naniwaiwai sending us to Hālawa Bay to experience the place where our ancestors first arrived in Hawaiʻi. Too many have forgotten our history. If you don't know where you come from, you don't know where you are. If you don't know where you are, you don't know where you're going. And if you don't know where you're going, you're probably going in the wrong direction.[54]

"The Hawaiian word *kupuna* is widely used to mean elder, grandparent or an older person. What is less recognized is the fact that the word has at least three distinct, but related meanings. First, a *kupuna* is an honored elder who has acquired enough life experience to become a family and community leader—a practitioner of Aloha (love), *pono* (righteousness), *mālama* (caring), and spirituality. In ancient times, they were teachers and caretakers of grandchildren, and that bond was especially strong. Even today, the *kūpuna* are expected to speak out and help make decisions on important issues for both the family and the community.

"*Kupuna* also means ancestor and includes the many generations before us, who by their spiritual wisdom and presence guide us through personal, family and community difficulties. We look to our *kūpuna* to help us find and fulfill our pathways through life. Included among our *kūpuna* are the family guardian spirits or *'aumākua* who take physical shape in the form of a *honu* (turtle), *manō* (shark) or a *pueo* (owl), and come to visit, warn and communicate with us.

"Finally, *kupuna* means the source, the starting point or the process of growth. This meaning is related to the notion that our direct forebearers and those of the distant past remain living treasures who continue to help us grow in numerous ways. They are a source of experience, knowledge, guidance, strength and inspiration to the next generations.[55]

"We must continually listen to the stories told by our *kūpuna* and the *'āina*. We must tell and retell these stories to our children and grandchildren, so they are never forgotten. Your grandchildren must tell them to their children and grandchildren. 'Knowledge is not complete until it is passed on.'[56] If you connect with the *kūpuna* and the *'āina* and listen to their stories, you will be filled with knowledge, power, and peace. If you only have knowledge from your generation, you will know very little.

"Similarly, there is much more to the stories than can be seen with your physical eyes or heard with your physical ears. You must see with your spiritual eyes. You must hear with your spiritual ears. You must feel with your spiritual heart. 'If all you know is what you see with your natural eyes and hear with your natural ears, you will not know very much.'"[57]

I enjoyed listening so much that I hardly realized we'd arrived back at Naniwaiwai's small home. We removed our sandals as we entered the *lanai* and immediately, the door opened and Naniwaiwai enthusiastically welcomed us with a hug, a kiss, and a warm Aloha. "How was Hālawa Bay?" she asked.

As we all found seats on the *lanai*, Manu answered, "I've been to Hālawa Bay before, but today was different. Although we were the only individuals on the beach, we were not alone. We were wrapped in the love of the *kūpuna* of Moloka'i."

Naniwaiwai replied, "You have an army of angels assisting you with your *kuleana*. I observed that some from this army were walking with you to the bay, while others were preparing the bay for your arrival and were there to welcome you to this sacred place."

She continued, "You have witnessed the fulfillment of the following promise of the Lord, 'I will go before your face. I will be on your right hand and on your left, and my Spirit shall be in your hearts, and mine angels round about you, to bear you up.'[58] Christ has also promised, 'I shall give my angels charge over you, to keep you in all your ways.'[59] When John was cast into prison, Jesus sent angels to minister to him.[60] Likewise, the Lord sends angels to minster to each of us.

"I feel great confidence that our *kūpuna*, who are now angels of the Most High, will go before you and prepare each place you will visit while you're here."

Naniwaiwai turned to me and asked, "Elder Taylor, did you see the angels?"

"I felt a great peace and warmth as we were at Hālawa Bay, and I felt the presence of heavenly spirits. I didn't see them, though," I answered.

"Elder Taylor, remember in the book of second Kings that the king sent horses, chariots, and a great host to capture Elisha. They came by night and encompassed the city. When the servant of Elisha awoke in the morning, he discovered they were surrounded by horses and chariots. With fear in his voice, he asked Elisha, 'Oh, my master, what are we to do?' Elisha answered, 'Fear not: for they that be with us are more than they that be with them.' And Elisha prayed saying, 'Lord, I pray thee, open his eyes, that he may see.' And the Lord opened the eyes of the young man; and he saw: and, behold, the mountain was full of horses and chariots of fire round about Elisha. Elder Taylor, please close your eyes as I pray."

I wasn't sure what Naniwaiwai was going to do, but I trusted her completely. I straightened in my chair and glanced at Manu as I bowed my head. His calm smile indicated to me that he was aware of what was going to happen.

Naniwaiwai raised her hand into the air, which I took as the signal to close my eyes.

"Lord, please open Elder Taylor's eyes that he may see."

I waited for more, but there was nothing else to her simple request. As my eyes slowly opened, my spiritual eyes were opened as well, and I saw that we were not only joined by angels on the *lanai* but that angels were surrounding Naniwaiwai's home. As I arose from my seat and walked to the edge of the *lanai* to look into the valley, I discovered that the valley was filled with angels as far as my eyes could see. I returned to my seat in wondrous awe.

"The gift of the ministering of angels is a gift of the Spirit available to all disciples of the Lord Jesus Christ," Naniwaiwai said, "both young and old, male and female. Talking with and receiving guidance, assistance, and protection from our angel ancestors has been a Hawaiian practice for centuries. Unfortunately, it's a gift rarely used in the world today."

She was right. To think that angels could be around my home, around my children strengthening them wherever they were—the very thought brought rest to my heart. Even while I was away, someone would be watching over my family. To think that everyone could have that reassurance made me want to shout it out.

Naniwaiwai opened her Book of Mormon. "The prophet Moroni wrote, 'Deny not the gifts of God, for they are many… and they are given by the manifestations of the Spirit of God unto men, to profit them. For behold, to one is given by the Spirit of God, that he may teach the word of wisdom; And to another, that he may teach the word of knowledge by the same Spirit; And to another, exceedingly great faith; and to another, the gifts of healing by the same Spirit; And again, to another, that he may work mighty miracles; And again, to another, that he may prophesy concerning all things; And again, to another, the beholding of angels and ministering spirits; And again, to another, all kinds of tongues; And again, to another, the interpretation of languages and of divers kinds of tongues. And all these gifts come by the Spirit of Christ; and they come unto every man severally, according as he will. And I would exhort you, my beloved brethren, that ye remember that every good gift cometh of Christ. And I would exhort you, my beloved brethren, that ye remember that he is the same yesterday, today, and forever, and that all these gifts of which I have spoken, which are spiritual, never will be done away, even as long as the world shall stand, only according to the unbelief of the children of men.'"[61]

Naniwaiwai pulled a page of notes from her scriptures and continued, "Elder Orson Pratt wrote, 'I have thought the reason why we have not enjoyed these gifts more fully is because we have not sought for them as diligently as we ought. I speak for one, I have not sought as diligently as I might have done. More than forty years have passed away since these promises were made. I have been blessed with some revelations and prophecies, and with dreams of things that have come to pass; but as to seeing things as a seer, and beholding heavenly things in open vision, I have not attained to these things. And who is to blame for this? Not the Lord; not brother Joseph— they are not to blame. And so it is with the promises made to you in your confirmations and endowments, and by the patriarchs, in your patriarchal blessings; we do not live up to our privileges as saints of God and elders of Israel; for though we receive many blessings that are promised to us, we do not receive them in their fullness, because we do not seek for them as diligently and faithfully as we should.'[62]

"The great missionary to these islands, George Q. Cannon, wrote, 'We cannot be the people that God designs we should be unless we seek after and obtain these spiritual gifts... It should be the constant prayer of all the Latter-day Saints for the Lord to give us those gifts that are suited to our condition.'"

I couldn't help but think about what gifts I should be pondering and pursuing. What had I been missing that the Lord was just waiting to bestow?

Naniwaiwai continued, "The prophet Moroni exhorts us to 'lay hold upon every good gift.'[63] And the Lord himself declares, 'Seek ye earnestly the best gifts, always remembering for what they are given.'[64] The beholding of angels and ministering spirits is a gift from Christ that you should diligently seek.

"The book of Job states, 'Those who came before us will teach you. They will teach you the wisdom of old.'[65] The light of your ancestors illuminates the path before you. To discover the path you are to follow, study the lives of your righteous ancestors. When you know where you come from, you will know where to go.

"The Hawaiian word for our guardian angels is 'aumākua. 'Aumakua is a personal guiding spirit, a family ancestor. Your 'aumākua are always at your side. Any time I'm in a difficult situation, I pause for a moment and ask for help. Every person has many family 'aumākua they can call upon for aid, but few people know how to work with their 'aumākua. They are there to help protect you and your family, to give you wisdom and vision to move successfully through life."[66]

Naniwaiwai's relationship with her relatives in the Spirit World was as real and active as her relationships with her living family. I knew I had much to learn and change.

"To understand the importance of genealogy and 'aumākua,

you must understand the Hawaiian word *mo'o*. The literal translation is dragon, but as you know, Hawaiian is a language of stories. You must know the stories to know the language.

"Elder Taylor, story is the life blood of Aloha. Story provides meaning, structure, and understanding. Story speaks to the heart. Story gives us eyes to see and a heart of Aloha. Story is truth and our way of knowing. Without air, our bodies die. Without story, our language, culture, and spirits die.

"*Mo'o* [dragon] is the story of family. The eyes of the dragon are to be fixed on truth. The front feet are the young children of the family. They are restless, always in motion. They move to and fro on the path. The middle feet are the parents. They are the center of the family and provide nourishment to the body and spirit of the children. The parents provide a home filled with Aloha. The hind feet of the dragon are the grandparents. They are prepared to help their children and grandchildren. They provide models of Aloha and provide guidance as they have the wisdom of living as a child and as a parent.

"The long tail of the dragon represents the ancestors that are now in the world of spirits. They are your *'aumākua*. They help the family in ways beyond the physical realm: caring, protecting, and guiding from the spirit world. The tail is the great stabilizer of the family. Each position is preparation for the next position, always moving on, always with the good of the family in mind. Each person is a small part of the whole, yet each part is integral and necessary for the whole to be complete."[67]

Naniwaiwai continued, "You can see the great importance of

mo'o as it's used throughout our language. *Mo'opuna* is the word for grandchildren. *Mo'olelo* is the word for story, history, and tradition. *Mo'olio* is a reference to your path. Understanding *mo'o* and its symbol of family connection and oneness is key to living with Aloha.

"*Mo'o kū'auhau* is the word for our genealogy chants. Each name in a genealogy chant carries the *mana* (spiritual power) of the ancestor. At birth, you begin to learn about the life of your ancestors and learn the chant of your genealogy. The longer the link of names in the chant, the longer the tail of your *mo'o*. With increased length comes increased stability, strength, and power.

I couldn't help but think of my own family. How far back could I recite? Could learning my genealogy bring stability and power to my family and children? While she spoke, I ached to look at my own family tree and start learning it by heart. I wanted those names to be part of me in the way Hawaiians made their ancestors part of their daily life.

I couldn't ponder longer as Naniwaiwai had more to say. "As you complete temple work for your ancestors, you connect with them. With each connection comes increased *mana*. As you connect with more and more of your ancestors, you have more and more *'aumākua* to call upon for Aloha, strength, guidance, empathy, and comfort.

"As I've learned about my ancestors and their lives, the names in the chants come alive to me. They are not just names. They are alive, and I speak with them. I love my ancestors. We're friends. I seek their guidance, counsel, and protection. They are as much a part of me and my life as the food I eat and the water I drink. My ancestors surround me with their light and their love. They listen to my problems and assist me through challenges and difficulties.

"The Book of Mormon shares with us about one of Alma's 'aumakua saying, 'And it came to pass that while [Alma] was journeying thither, being weighed down with sorrow, wading through much tribulation and anguish of soul... behold an angel of the Lord appeared unto him, saying: Blessed art thou, Alma; therefore, lift up thy head and rejoice, for thou hast great cause to rejoice; for thou hast been faithful in keeping the commandments of God from the time which thou receivedst thy first message from him. Behold, I am he that delivered it unto you.'[68]

"The same angel who had visited Alma with the sons of Mosiah came to strengthen Alma. He is one of his guardian angels. When Alma was weighed down with sorrow, his 'aumakua came to strengthen him.

"Elder Taylor, did Manu show you the poster in town that reads, 'Keep calm and call on your ancestors'?"

"No," I replied. "I definitely would have remembered that one."

"I think this is sound advice," said Naniwaiwai. "When you're filled with darkness and despair, ask your ancestors to share their light and hope. When you fall on your face, ask your ancestors to help you up. When a burden is weighing you down, call upon your ancestors to lift you up.

"What the mainland would call death, I call a new birth. I don't use the words dead or died. Instead, I say, 'They are now in spirit.' I know that life continues in a new realm of spirits. The transition from our mortal existence to the spirit world is no more a death than the transition from the pre-mortal world to our life on earth. Our relationships with our grandparents and great grandparents don't end at death. These relationships continue. The prophets have taught us that the Spirit World is on this earth.[69] Our ancestors surround us.

"Chanting the names of your ancestors is a way to remember them, to give them thanks, and to strengthen your relationship and connection with them. My family chant connects with fifty generations. My grandchildren's chant contains fifty-two generations, as it includes my generation and the generation of my children."

Naniwaiwai stood and began to chant. Each word left her lips with a familiarity filled with love. The names of her ancestors floated from her mouth as a beautiful song. Her chant connected heaven and earth. Tears streamed down my cheeks as her chant carried the message of *moʻo* deep into my heart.

When she completed her chant, Naniwaiwai sat down. I grabbed a tissue from the box sitting on the small end table on the *lanai*.

"Naniwaiwai, may I have a copy of your family chant?" I asked. I didn't have my own genealogy chart with me, but that didn't mean I couldn't start learning from Naniwaiwai's.

"This chant isn't written on paper, Elder Taylor. It's written on my heart."

Naniwaiwai turned to Manu and said, "I think it's time for you to take Elder Taylor to see the *moʻo*. You will need to take clothes you can swim in."

CHAPTER 11
MOʻOULA FALLS

"Nature is one of our greatest healers."

- Linda Kaholokai

I'd packed my swim trunks. It was an island after all, but I didn't know what she had in mind. Manu gave me a knowing smile before we went and put on our swimsuits. I'd also learned after I'd put on my sandals that we'd be hiking up the valley. Manu assured me my sandals would be fine. After giving Naniwaiwai a hug and a kiss, we began walking up the dirt road.

"So, you're taking me to see a dragon?" I asked curiously.

"Yes, I'm taking you to the *moʻo* of Hālawa Valley," answered Manu.

I smiled with excitement and anticipation.

"The hike is about two miles and will include crossing a river several times and climbing over rocks and fallen trees. Hālawa Valley is one of the few remaining pristine valleys in Hawaiʻi. Naniwaiwai and the other families living here have worked hard to preserve it. This valley has been the home of thousands of Hawaiians over the centuries.

"Today, fewer than twenty people call Hālawa Valley home. There is no internet, no cell service, and no modern plumbing. While many view this as a negative, Naniwaiwai wouldn't want it any other way. *ʻĀina* is a gift from God and provides everything we need. You take care of the *ʻāina*, and the *ʻāina* will take care of you. You are a servant and steward of the *ʻāina*. The *ʻāina* isn't something to master or own. *ʻĀina* is to be respected, revered, and served. This is summed up in the Hawaiian saying, '*He aliʻi i nō ka ʻāina, he kauā nō ke kanaka,*' which translates to English as 'The land is the chief. Man is the servant.'"

We came to a small trail that veered off from the dirt road. The trees and shrubs were thick on both sides, creating a wall of green that felt as though we had stepped into a different world.

"Elder Taylor, as we hike through the forest, you will see *heiau* (temples), ancient rock walls, home foundations, and ancient taro terraces that were built by our ancestors. While there are no mortals living in this part of the valley today, it's still the home of our ancestors. It's important we get their permission to visit."

Manu pulled a conch shell from his backpack and blew long and loud. Shortly after Manu finished blowing, another long and loud sound reverberated from deep in the forest.

"That sounded like another conch shell," I said. "Who is that?"

"I'm glad to see you have ears to hear, Elder Taylor. Few people hear the sound of our ancestors' conch giving us permission to enter," Manu replied.

It was clear he had experienced this many times before, but it was a first for me. The hair on my arm rose, not in alarm but because of a feeling that we were guided by angels.

Manu continued, "To prepare to enter the valley, we should inhale deeply and say *'ha'* as we exhale. This is a time to ask the *'āina* for permission to enter. This ancient protocol is a reminder of the sacred breath of life infused in God's creation and prepares us to connect with the *'āina*."

We began to inhale deeply with the whisper of "*haaaaaaaaaaaaaaaaaa*" as we exhaled. The breathing cleared my mind, calmed my soul, and wrapped me in the Holy Spirit.

Following a few minutes of breathing, we entered into the mature tropical forest. It was still and quiet, except for the sounds of birds singing and the rustling of the leaves. After a few minutes of hiking, we came to a stream that we needed to cross. I paused for a moment mid-stream, gazing up and down to take in the beauty of the valley. The stream was lined with trees and gray boulders of various shapes and sizes. Branches grew over the water, creating a beautiful green canopy. The sound of the water flowing over and through the rocks was soothing and magical.

As we continued hiking, I was amazed at the numerous structures, rock walls, and *kalo* terraces throughout the valley. It was clear that a large, thriving community once existed here. Manu provided insightful commentary on each of the sites we passed. The sky still shone a brilliant blue, but clouds moved in and provided shade where the trees did not.

After about two hours of walking and talking, a magnificent waterfall suddenly came into view. The majesty of the falls increased as we climbed closer to it. We stopped at the edge of the pool below the waterfall and watched as the water flowed down the high cliff and thundered into a beautiful, large, circular pool.

"How tall is this waterfall?" I inquired.

"It's about 250 feet. This is one of six major falls in the valley. The falls flow into the stream that runs down the valley. It's the same stream we waded across to get to the beach at Hālawa Bay earlier this morning. Do you see the *moʻo*?"

I looked around, but I didn't see a dragon anywhere. I scanned the mountain as well as the cave openings in the cliffs that surrounded the falls. I looked into the water. I didn't see anything.

"Manu, I don't see the *moʻo*. Will you please help me?" I wasn't sure what I should be looking for.

Manu offered a chant in Hawaiian. Suddenly a burst of rain poured down, cleansing the mountain. Manu resumed his chant. The rain stopped and the clouds cleared. I was surprised to see Manu's chant direct the weather.

"Now, do you see the *moʻo*?" Manu asked.

As I looked at the mountain above the waterfall, rays of sun illuminated a shape on the mountain that was clearly a dragon.

"Yes. I see the *moʻo*," I said with a smile.

"Hawaiians have come to this place to share the story of *moʻo* for over two thousand years. They come here to connect with their *ʻaumākua*. They bring their children and grandchildren here to connect them to their ancestors and to teach them the way of Aloha.

"On some maps, you will see this place called Moaʻula Falls. Somewhere along the lines, someone changed the 'o' to 'a' and it was recorded as Moa'ula instead of Mo'oula. *Moa* means chicken in Hawaiian. Ancient Hawaiians didn't have chickens. Those who know the chants and songs of Hālawa know that this is Mo'oula Falls, not Moa'ula Falls. One of the residents who was born and raised in this valley, Uncle Pilipo, has worked diligently to ensure the falls are properly called Mo'oula on maps and in books, chants, and songs. It's important that the names are preserved correctly because if you change the name, you change the story. Are you ready for a swim?" Manu asked.

I nodded and said, "Yes."

"First, you must ask permission from the Creator of heaven and earth, the *'āina*, and the *mo'o*, who is a guardian of this sacred waterfall and pool. As you have learned, a chant is much more than words that are spoken. It's a *pule* (prayer) to God. It's to come from the heart. There is power and meaning in the tones, breath, vibrations, and cadence. There is power and meaning in the motions of the body and hands.

"To begin, bow your head and shoulders and look between your feet."

I looked to Manu and mirrored his stance.

"Now, find the smallest particle you can see and begin to focus on it."

I found a small rock and focused my gaze.

"This is to remind you how small you are, of your nothingness. After the Lord showed Moses a vision of heaven and earth, Moses declared, 'I know that man is nothing, which thing I never had supposed.'[70]

"Now, begin to raise both your gaze and arms upward until you are looking and reaching into the heavens. As you look up, everything is larger. See the vastness of God's creation. You're connected with all of it. God's creation isn't billions of individual pieces and parts, but one great whole. What you do to the 'āina, you do to yourself. When you feel you're an individual of great importance, look between your feet and remember your nothingness. When you feel insignificant or alone, look up and remember you're a child of God."

Manu taught me the words of the chant. Though I knew a little Hawaiian, the words didn't slip off my tongue as easily as I would have hoped. It was awkward, but the concentration it required cleared my mind. Manu had me practice the chant many times, working on my tone, inflexions, and pronunciation.

"I think you're ready now," Manu declared.

We began the chant together with our hands raised high above our heads as we looked into the sky. We repeated the chant as we lowered our heads and our hands toward the ground. We offered the chant three times.

After a period of silence, we descended quietly into the pure, fresh water. The water grew deeper and deeper as I walked toward the waterfall. The water was over my head within twenty yards of the shore, and I began to tread with my feet and hands working in unison. I was drawn to the waterfall and continued to swim until I reached its base. I treaded water under the falls, allowing the water to pour over my head and shoulders. I swam to the side, holding onto a nook in the cliff, watching and listening to the water flow down the cliff and crash into the pool.

We swam for about thirty minutes and then found a place on the rocks to bask in the sun.

"How do you feel, Elder Taylor?" Manu asked.

"I feel energized." It was the only answer that seemed appropriate.

Manu smiled. "Yes, that's a good word—energized. As you connect with the *ʻāina*, you are invigorated. You're filled with energy and healing. When you connect with *ʻāina*, you connect with God. The touch of nature is the touch of God. The touch of God renews, lifts, and heals. You have been filled with the *mana* of Moʻoula Falls and touched by its healing and strengthening power.

"The Hawaiian word *lomi* means healing touch. The tactile touch of nature is extremely important. Your body needs to walk barefoot on the grass and the beach. Your body needs to swim in lakes, rivers, and oceans. Your hands need to touch and embrace the earth. *ʻĀina* is sacred and nourishes your body and spirit. When you are touched by nature, you are touched by God, and there's healing power in God's touch. You need to connect with *ʻāina* as much as you need food and water.

"You don't have to live in Hawaiʻi to connect with nature, Elder Taylor. God's creations are everywhere. Have you heard of the David Suzuki Foundation?"

I hadn't.

"The David Suzuki Foundation challenged more than ten thousand participants in Canada to get out into nature for thirty minutes a day for thirty consecutive days. The foundation released the results of their study saying, 'We found that participants in the 30×30 Nature Challenge almost doubled their time spent outside during the month and reduced their screen time by about 4.5 hours per week. They reported significant increases in their sense of well-being, feeling more vitality and energy while feelings of stress, negativity, and sleep disturbances were all reduced.'

"We live in a world that has become very disconnected from the 'āina. Many of our physical troubles and stresses are caused by a deficiency of nature. What's often diagnosed as a disorder is just a symptom of nature deficiency. The treatment that's needed isn't a pill, but more time connecting with nature. I think we would make far greater progress with our children if we addressed nature deficient disorder instead of attention deficient disorder.

"I think it's time to head back to Naniwaiwai's for dinner," Manu said. "I don't know about you, but I'm starving. I'll let Naniwaiwai know we're heading back."

"Manu, I thought you said there are no cell phones in Hālawa. How are you going to let her know?" I asked perplexed.

Manu smiled. "I forget how much you still have to learn, Elder Taylor. Hawaiians have a technology much more advanced than that of cell phones, and they have had it for two thousand years. We're able to talk spirit-to-spirit. This was a common practice among our ancestors.[71] It's far less common today, but there are still a few who have developed this gift of the Spirit. What would you like for dinner? I'll let her know."

I didn't want my confusion and disbelief to show. My mouth hung open as I pondered this radical idea. I wasn't sure what to think, but answered, "Well, two of my favorites are teriyaki chicken and bananas in coconut milk."

"That sounds good to me," Manu replied. His face remained calm, but I could tell he wasn't quite with me. There was no nod of the head or blink of the eye to indicate he'd sent any kind of message. Yet, he seemed confident that both dishes would be waiting for us.

We talked story as we made our way down the valley. Our trip down was much quicker than the journey up and we arrived back at Naniwaiwai's home in about an hour. As we took off our sandals, I smelled a wonderful aroma coming from inside, and my stomach began to rumble in anticipation.

Naniwaiwai came out to the *lanai* and greeted each of us with a *honi*. As we entered the home, Naniwaiwai said, "You're right on time. The teriyaki chicken is ready to come out of the oven."

I looked to Manu. The question, "How did you do that?" written all over my face. He shrugged and followed Naniwaiwai into the house.

We helped Naniwaiwai set the table (the bowl of *poi* still remaining at the center) and made the final preparations for dinner. We held hands, standing in a circle and we each offered words of prayer, praise, and gratitude. When we finished our prayers, we took our seats. I was excited for the teriyaki chicken and, of course, there was also a large bowl of bananas cooked in coconut milk.

After discussing the experiences of the day, we talked story and laughed while we continued to enjoy the *ono* (delicious) dinner. It was a pleasant evening, but I couldn't help but feel a little awkward about the situation.

As we helped clean the kitchen, I said, "Naniwaiwai, I hope I didn't cause you trouble and stress with my request for teriyaki chicken and bananas with coconut milk. When Manu asked what I wanted for dinner, I was really hungry, and those two things sounded *ono* to me. We were miles away with no cell phone, so I thought my request was just an impossible wish."

Naniwaiwai smiled. "I was grateful for the request. Cooking food that brings you joy brings me joy and is a way for me to show you my love."

Her words brought tears to my eyes. "I love you, Naniwaiwai," I said as I embraced her.

Naniwaiwai squeezed me back. "I love you, too."

CHAPTER 12

HIKE TO MOUNTAIN HEIAU

"One's destination is never a place but rather a new way of looking at things."

- Henry Miller

I awoke in the morning at sunrise. The sounds of two people already awake and moving around the house acted as the motivation I needed to not fall back asleep. I was still adjusting to the time change. I got ready for the day and spent time in prayer, scripture study, and meditation. There was so much to contemplate and ponder. I thought about everything Manu told me at the waterfall and knew there was more to it. Being here in this place with a rich spiritual history made me want to learn more.

After finishing our breakfast, we sat on the *lanai* talking story. As our discussion progressed, Naniwaiwai said, "Elder Taylor, yesterday you asked for a copy of my *mo'o kū'auhau* (genealogy chant). I've given much thought to your request. The many *mo'o kū'auhau* recorded in the scriptures were brought to my mind. It's not by chance that several of the ancient books of scriptures begin with a *mo'o kū'auhau*. The principle of *mo'o* has been taught by God to his people since the beginning of time. Today, many skim through or skip over the genealogies recorded in the Bible and the Book of Mormon. They have forgotten the importance of *moʻo*."

Naniwaiwai handed me a few sheets of paper. I examined the paper to see a handwritten list of her family chant.

She continued, "To ensure this chant is preserved for my posterity and as an example to other families throughout the world, I felt I should give you my *moʻo kūʻauhau* in writing. But, please remember that there is far greater *mana* when it's chanted from the heart than when it's read from a paper."

As I held these sacred pages in my hands, the Spirit enveloped me and bore witness to me of their importance.

"Elder Taylor, although many Latter-day Saints have done extensive genealogy work, their work isn't truly complete until they create a *moʻo kūʻauhau* and chant it from their hearts and their children and their grandchildren chant it from their hearts."

Her words struck me. My children had seen my genealogy chart, but had they ever read it? Had I told them about each of the names that made our family tree? In my mind, I made a commitment that when I returned to Idaho, I would work with my family to create our *moʻo kūʻauhau* and learn to regularly chant our genealogy.

Naniwaiwai continued, "I've felt that today, I should take you to a *heiau* that sits at the highest point of the Hālawa mountains. The climb is extremely steep, and the trails have been overgrown for many generations. You will need to take lunch as it's an all-day journey. Are you up to the challenge?"

My eyebrows raised. Was this 107-year-old woman really asking if I was up to the challenge? However, I could tell Manu was hiding a smile, so I nodded along with him. Naniwaiwai directed us to a map of the valley that was hanging on the wall of her *lanai*, pointing to the location of the *heiau* on the map.

"The angels will prepare the way before you and provide direction, and you will be drawn to the great *mana* that radiates from this location."

Manu and I quickly changed into pants, long sleeve t-shirts, and hiking shoes. We packed our lunches, gave Naniwaiwai a hug and kiss goodbye, and began our adventure.

Our hike started as the day before with a walk down the dirt road. We followed the road for about a mile until we came to a game trail off the road. We followed the same protocol we had followed on our hike to the falls, with Manu blowing his conch and time spent breathing.

"We'll use the game trails as much as we can as we make our way up the mountain," Manu said. "Many deer and wild boars live throughout the valley. In the 1860s, spotted deer were introduced to the island of Moloka'i as a gift from Hong Kong to King Kamehameha V. The wild boars have been here much longer. It's believed that they were brought to Hawai'i by early Polynesians. Another species of pig was introduced to Hawai'i by the Europeans in the eighteenth century following Captain Cook's visits to the islands."

Manu paused on the trail and pointed ahead as he said, "Elder Taylor, have you noticed the owl that's guiding us?"

I reluctantly admitted that I hadn't. Manu pointed toward a tree ahead of us, and I caught sight of the beautiful creature. Her small body was easy to miss amongst the trees, but once I knew what I was looking for, I felt a little sheepish that I hadn't noticed her presence. I connected with her wide, intense stare, and immediately knew I was witnessing something sacred.

"This is one of our *'aumākua* who has come to guide us to the *heiau*. It's very common for *'aumākua* to manifest themselves as an animal."

I tried to formulate words to describe what I was feeling, but no words came. Though it was my first time seeing the Hawaiian owl, a connection seemed to stretch from her to me and probably to Manu, too. She was as much a member of our party as either of us.

Manu continued, "The *pueo* is native to Hawai'i and is a subspecies of the short-eared owl. While our *'aumākua* may appear as a hawk, sea turtle, shark or other animal, the most common form taken by our *'aumākua* is that of a *pueo*. Because of this, the *pueo* is greatly respected and protected in Hawai'i."

I stood silently for a time, watching this majestic bird, overwhelmed by her magnificence. Manu finally broke the silence and said, "You can be told about *'aumākua* and read about *'aumākua* all you want, but until you experience your *'aumākua*, you will not fully understand. Words are inadequate to describe the experience of being guided by your *'aumākua*. You learn and know truth through experience."

Manu began walking toward our *pueo*. As we approached the owl, it flew ahead and landed on a tree along the trail. This pattern continued as we made our way up the mountain.

After about an hour of following our *pueo* along game trails, our guide landed on a tree that was no longer on the trails. We followed, weaving through the trees and brush of the forest. Our hike had been a steady upward climb with the steepness increasing as we progressed. It now took much more exertion to make each step. With the heat of the day increasing, drops of sweat began dripping from my face.

We found a place to sit and paused for a moment to rest. "Elder Taylor, I'm glad there is no trail to this *heiau*."

"Why is that, Manu?" I asked, as I wiped the sweat from my brow.

"Many of our *heiau* have been destroyed and desecrated. It's a blessing that this *heiau* is difficult to reach so that it's hidden from the world."

"How much farther do you think we have to hike?" I tried not to let the effects of my exertions show, but my deep breaths may have revealed the true nature of my question.

Manu looked around and answered, "My guess is that we have another hour to reach the summit."

The entire time we rested, our *pueo* perched on a tree a few feet away from us. It was wonderful to be so close to this majestic bird and feel her love, strength, and wisdom. Our *pueo* resumed flight, continuing as our guide as we got to our feet.

Our steady pace moved us onward, but we weren't rushed or hurried. The time walking in nature, immersed in the beauty and wonder of the forest was edifying to both our bodies and spirits. As I watched our *pueo* fly ahead of us, I suddenly saw a second *pueo* join our guide.

"Did you see the second *pueo*?" I asked.

"Yes," Manu smiled, "you're learning to see. We must be getting close."

As we followed the two *pueo*, two more flew in and joined them.

We soon followed four owls as we completed our final steps to the summit. There was a small clearing on the mountain and the *heiau* came into sight. I watched the *pueo* fly to the *heiau*. Each bird landed on a corner of the temple. The birds faced away from the interior of the *heiau* and appeared to stand as keepers and protectors of this sacred edifice.

I felt as if I had been transported back in time to ancient Hawai'i. This temple was a light on a hill. The trees, flowers, and bushes surrounding the temple were superb. The view of the valleys and ocean was inspiring. The temple was in such magnificent condition I didn't think it could possibly be the same one built by the ancient Hawaiians.

Turning to Manu I inquired, "Has this temple been reconstructed?"

Smiling, Manu answered, "No. This temple is over a thousand years old. It was built by our *kūpuna* with a divine design that will last through the millennium. It has been preserved and maintained by our *kūpuna* for centuries.

I instinctively walked toward the temple. Manu placed his arm in front of me, stopping my progress. "Elder Taylor, before we approach the walls of the temple, we must offer our thanks and praise to God."

"Of course, Manu. I'm sorry. I forgot the order of things."

"It's quite all right, Elder Taylor," he said, smiling patiently.

"Eagerness to be in the house of the Lord is never a bad thing. Are you familiar with the 43rd Psalm?"

I thought for a second before shaking my head no.

"The 43rd Psalm reads, 'O send out thy light and thy truth: let them lead me;'[72] 'let them bring me to your holy mountain, to the place where you dwell.'[73] 'I will go to the altar of God...my joy and my delight. I will praise you...O God.'"[74]

"It's beautiful," I said quieting my voice. "I don't ever recall hearing it."

"I agree, Elder Taylor. It's not only beautiful, but it's quite descriptive of our journey today. We've been led to a holy mountain. God has sent His light and truth to lead us. We must express our thanks and praise His glorious name. Are you familiar with *oli*?"

"*Oli* is the Hawaiian word for chant, isn't it?"

"Yes. Very good, Elder Taylor. Chants have been an important part of worship since the beginning of time. The LDS hymn book is filled with chants. The hymn "I Heard the Bells on Christmas Day" contains the *oli* 'peace on earth, good will to men.' The lyrics read, 'A voice, a chime, a chant sublime, Of peace on earth, good will to men!'

"The lyrics of the hymn 'He is Risen' directs us to 'Chant our Lord's triumphant lay.' You're to chant the good news of the Lord Jesus Christ and chant your gratitude and praise for His wondrous works."

Manu took a few deep breaths and began to chant. His voice was as powerful as a lion, yet soft as a breeze. Throughout the chant, breath elegantly fell from his lips. The words flowed from his heart with vibrations that penetrated my soul. As Manu chanted, I was warmed by the Spirit.

Manu turned to me and said, "Now, it's your turn."

I hesitated. "I'm happy to give it a try."

"You will do fine, Elder Taylor. With practice, your chanting will improve and increase in *mana*, rhythm, and Aloha. The gift of voice is one of God's greatest gifts. Just as Christ's breath (*ha*) gives you life, your chants give words life. Breath gives words love, power, and meaning. The words, inflections, vibrations, and tones of a chant are selected with great care and consideration. *Oli* is used to communicate with God, *kūpuna*, family, friends, and nature."

"Manu, I caught some of the words in your chant, but I didn't understand it fully. What did you say in your *oli*? What do I say in mine?"

Manu answered, "An *oli* is much more than the words that are spoken. Chants are like a parable so there are multiple layers of meaning. Chants are alive. The *oli* I just shared gives thanks and praise to God. When *oli* is used to communicate with God, it's a prayer. Elder Taylor, even though you lived in Hawai'i for two years as a missionary, I bet you never followed the directive found in Isaiah 42:11-12."

I shrugged my shoulders, not sure where Manu was going with this statement. "I love the book of Isaiah," I replied, "but I don't recall this specific passage."

Manu continued, "Isaiah declares, 'Let them shout from the top of the mountains. Let them give glory unto the Lord and declare his praise in the islands.' Today, you can fulfill these words of the prophet

Isaiah, Elder Taylor. I'll teach you the short Hawaiian *oli* of Psalms 135:3, 'Praise the Lord for the Lord is good.'"

Manu performed the *oli* in full and then offered the *oli* one word at a time, having me repeat each word back to him. I tried to emulate his tone, inflections, rhythm, and power. If my pronunciation was off, he would repeat the word again and again until my emulation was close to his. After rehearsing the complete chant several times together, the chant began to flow more easily from my lips.

Looking me in the eyes, Manu said, "You're ready, Elder Taylor. It's time for you to perform the *oli* alone."

I offered a silent prayer, took a couple of deep breaths and began, *"E halelu aku ia Iehova, no ka mea, ua maikai o Iehova."*

Manu smiled. "Well done, Elder Taylor, well done. How does it feel?"

"I felt a power and energy stir within me that carried the words from within my body to the heavens," I answered. "It felt as if a part of my body and spirit that had been asleep was awakened."

Manu nodded. "Now, you're beginning to understand *oli*. You have awakened the power of *ha*. God designed your body to chant. Chanting connects you with the heavens. Chanting renews, heals, and strengthens the body and the spirit.

"Chanting is about connection. There are *oli* to connect with God. There are *oli* to connect with ancestors and family. There are *oli* to connect with strangers and friends. There are *oli* to reconcile and connect with enemies. There are *oli* to connect with animals. There are *oli* to connect with the *'āina*. Are you ready to approach the temple?"

"Yes," I nodded.

We walked toward the walls of the temple. The *pueo* still perched on each corner of the *heiau*. There was no entrance on the sides of the temple within our view, so we walked around it. As we rounded the corner, I was stunned to see Naniwaiwai sitting silent and looking in the distance.

Naniwaiwai's attention turned to us and she greeted us with a warm, "Aloha."

"Aloha," Manu and I replied in unison.

Still trying to recover from my shock, I blurted out, "How did you get here?"

Manu and I had hiked for several hours up the steep mountain. While we didn't rush, we maintained a good, steady pace. She was in excellent shape for a 107-year-old, but there was simply no way she could have ascended this mountain faster than we did.

Naniwaiwai smiled and answered, "I'll answer that question in a minute, Elder Taylor. Before I answer your questions, I would like to add a few thoughts on praise and *oli*. Please come and sit with me."

After Manu, Naniwaiwai and I all sat in a circle on the ground facing the temple, Naniwaiwai spoke.

"When the Protestant missionaries arrived in Hawai'i in the early 1800s, they banned many Hawaiian practices, thinking these practices conflicted with the gospel of Jesus Christ. One of those was *oli*. These early missionaries didn't understand the difference between culture and gospel. Since *oli* wasn't a part of their culture, they assumed it wasn't a part of the gospel of Christ and forbade it as an apostate practice. Elder Taylor, we must not make the same mistake these missionaries made.

"It's very important to distinguish the difference between cultural practices and the truths of Christ's gospel. One such example would be prayer. It's an eternal truth that God is our Father and that He is willing and anxious to communicate with each of His children, and that He longs to have each of His children talk with Him. We call communication with God prayer, but prayer can take on many forms. There are countless ways to pray to God and these practices vary from culture to culture and family to family.

"The Hawaiians prayed through chants, music, and dance. The Western missionaries banned praying through both *oli* and *hula* because these prayer practices didn't align with their culture. The purpose of prayer is to build a relationship with God. I believe the Hawaiians were much more effective in accomplishing this through *hula* and *oli* than the Western missionaries were with their verbal prayers. I believe the missionaries could have learned much about prayer and having a relationship with God from the Hawaiian culture, but instead they imposed their culture and their practices of prayer on the Hawaiians.

"Another area where there are often cultural differences is in how we praise God. We owe everything we have and are to Almighty God, so it's important that we show Him our reverence, respect, honor and gratitude. This is called praise. Wherever the gospel of Jesus Christ is lived, you will find people praising God. The Bible, Book of Mormon, and Doctrine and Covenants are filled with examples of praise from both individuals and groups. Nephi wrote, 'I did praise him all the day long.'[75] Nephi also instructs us that once you receive the gift of the Holy Ghost, you can 'speak with the tongue of angels, and shout praises unto the Holy One of Israel.'[76] The book of Ether states, 'The Brother of Jared did...praise the Lord all the day long; and when the night came, they did not cease to praise the Lord.'[77]

"We should seek to follow the examples of praising God provided by Nephi and the Brother of Jared. I believe some members of The Church of Jesus Christ of Latter-day Saints today think praise is something done in other Christian denominations. In fact, if you were to shout praises to God in a Latter-day Saint community on the mainland, you would most likely receive some strange looks and may even get called into the Bishop's office.

"Many have suppressed the gifts of the Holy Ghost and have failed to shout praise to the Holy One of Israel. They suppress the gift of *ha*. We need to make sure we don't make the same mistake as the early Christian missionaries and suppress activities that align with the truths of the gospel of Jesus Christ simply because they don't align with Church cultural traditions.

"Elder Taylor, while you can freely praise the Lord and chant praises and thanks to His name while you're here in Hālawa Valley, this behavior may not be accepted at first when you return to Idaho. Be of good cheer, though. When you clash with a church culture that isn't in harmony with the gospel of Jesus Christ, remember that you're in good company. Jesus was in constant conflict with the church culture of His day. He lived His gospel in defiance of the culture of the church. The church leaders constantly criticized Him and tried to stop Him.

"Today, there continues to be Pharisees within Christ's restored church who perpetuate, protect, and preserve church culture that's in conflict with the gospel of Christ. We must bravely live the gospel of Christ, especially when it's contrary to the Church culture. We must provide an example of gospel-centered living and work to change the Church culture to more closely align with the gospel of Jesus Christ.

"When you find yourself trying to determine who and what to follow, simply remember that Jesus Christ is your King and your Leader. You will answer to Him, and He will be your righteous judge in eternity."

The Spirit was palpable as Naniwaiwai finished speaking. The three of us sat in silence for some time, drinking in the beauty of the Spirit.

"Thank you, Naniwaiwai, for sharing your insight and counsel with us," I finally said. "You have the gift of wisdom."

Smiling, she replied, "Thank you, Elder Taylor. My ancestors and I have learned much over the past two thousand years."

CHAPTER 13

YOU CAN DO ALL THINGS

"All things are possible for the one who believes." [78]

- Jesus Christ

We sat in the comfort of silence. I could still see the *pueo* and wondered who else they'd guided to this very spot. I had so many thoughts moving through my mind that I probably could have sat for the rest of the day, but there was still one nagging question.

"Naniwaiwai, are you ready to answer my question about how you got here? No offense, but there is no way you could walk faster than we did."

Naniwaiwai chuckled. "Yes, Elder Taylor. I'm ready to answer your question, but are you ready for my answer?"

I paused and pondered for a moment. She patiently waited until I nodded that I was ready.

"I traveled here by faith, Elder Taylor."

"By faith?" I knew a lot of things could happen by faith, even climbing a mountain, but that didn't make it any easier to understand. "What does that mean? How does that work?"

"When you move with the physical body, Elder Taylor, it takes many steps to get to the top of the mountain. When you move like the angels, however, it only takes faith as the grain of a mustard seed. Moving objects and traveling by faith was a common practice among the ancient Hawaiian *kumu*[79] (teachers) but it's a practice that has long been forgotten.

"I desire to build within my children and my grandchildren the belief that travel by faith is possible. In order to do this, I needed two witnesses to be able to testify that I did indeed travel by faith to this mountain *heiau*. If my children and grandchildren don't believe moving objects or traveling like angels is possible, they will not even attempt to try these things. Belief is the first step to doing the impossible. For all things are possible to those who believe."[80]

I marveled as I looked into Naniwaiwai's eyes. She radiated wisdom, humility, and strength. It was an honor to be in her presence and to learn from her.

With a grin on my face I asked, "Your middle name wouldn't happen to be Yoda, would it?"

Chuckling, Manu answered before she could respond, "No, Elder Taylor. There is no Y or D in the Hawaiian alphabet, but the force is strong with her."

Naniwaiwai smiled and said, "The power to move objects is a skill that has been taught and used by Hawaiians for two thousand years. As a young girl, the training by my *kumu* included contests of concentration such as moving objects. Such stories are now considered by many to be untrue. When I was growing up, it was everyday practice.[81] It was part of our training as disciples of the Lord

Jesus Christ.

"The Lord says, 'If ye have faith as a grain of mustard seed, ye shall say unto this mountain, Remove hence to yonder place; and it shall remove; and nothing shall be impossible unto you.'[82] If, by faith, you can move mountains, why do you think it strange that, by faith, a person would be able to move to the top of a mountain?"

"When you put it that way, it makes a lot more sense," I admitted.

Pointing to a boulder in the temple wall that was the size of a pickup truck, Naniwaiwai asked, "How do you think our ancestors got that stone to the top of this mountain?"

"By faith?" I answered.

"Yes, Elder Taylor. They used their *mana* (spiritual power) to move boulders to the top of these mountains."

As Naniwaiwai said these words, the Spirit witnessed to me that what she had said was true.

Manu interjected, "You have experienced the importance of asking permission during your trip. When the Hawaiians built temples, they would get the permission of the rocks before they moved them, first asking the rock if it approved of being used as part of the temple. They only used rocks in their temples that wanted to be a part of the temple and that had agreed to be a part of the temple. God has created the rocks, plants, and animals for the use of man, but they should be used with permission, not by force. The Lord says in the Doctrine and Covenants, 'And it pleaseth God that he hath given all these things unto man; for unto this end were they made to be used, with judgment, not to excess, neither by extortion.'[83] What's extortion? It's the practice of obtaining something through force. When you use a rock, plant, or animal without their permission, it is extortion."

Naniwaiwai nodded in agreement and continued, "Many have wondered how large rocks were moved to the top of mountains in Hawai'i and in other places throughout the world such as Easter Island and Machu Picchu. Oral histories passed down from my ancestors tell the story of how they used *mana* (spiritual power) to build this temple and others. I believe the large stones on Easter Island and at Machu Picchu may have been moved by *mana* as well."[84]

I sat in awe and wonder as I looked at the large stones used to build this temple. "May I touch one of the stones of the temple?" I asked.

"Yes, Elder Taylor, but not yet. I would like to share a story with you first."

Naniwaiwai opened her scriptures and began to read, "'Jesus constrained his disciples to get into a ship, and to go before him unto the other side while he sent the multitudes away. And when he had sent the multitudes away, he went up into a mountain apart to pray: and when the evening was come, he was there alone. But the ship was now in the midst of the sea, tossed with waves: for the wind was contrary. And in the fourth watch of the night Jesus went unto them, walking on the sea. And when the disciples saw him walking on the sea, they were troubled, saying, It is a spirit; and they cried out for fear. But straightway Jesus spake unto them, saying, Be of good cheer; it is I; be not afraid. And Peter answered him and said, Lord, if it be thou, bid me come unto thee on the water. And he said, Come.

And when Peter was come down out of the ship, he walked on the water, to go to Jesus. But when he saw the wind boisterous, he was afraid; and beginning to sink, he cried, saying, Lord, save me. And immediately Jesus stretched forth his hand, and caught him, and said unto him, O thou of little faith, wherefore didst thou doubt?'[85]

"Elder Taylor, many key lessons can be learned from this story. Have you ever wondered why Peter would ask to get out of the boat? Why would Peter ask to go to Jesus when Jesus was coming to get into the boat?

"That's an interesting question," I answered. "I can't say that it's one I've asked myself before."

Naniwaiwai continued, "I pondered on this question for several days. After much pondering, the spiritual impression came to me that Jesus had been teaching and telling His followers that they were to do the miracles they saw Him perform."

Naniwaiwai flipped the pages of her scriptures and read, "'These twelve Jesus sent forth, and commanded them, saying...Heal the sick, cleanse the lepers, raise the dead, cast out devils: freely ye have received, freely give.'[86] They were to do the mighty miracles they saw the Savior do. He told them that with faith, they were to perform miracles in His name and that nothing would be impossible to them. Not only did Jesus tell them to perform the miracles they saw, He told them they would perform even greater miracles."

Naniwaiwai read from another passage of scripture, "'Verily, verily, I say unto you, He that believeth on me, the works that I do shall he do also; and greater works than these shall he do; because I go unto my Father. And whatsoever ye shall ask in my name, that will I do.'[87]

"When Peter saw Christ walking on the water, he had faith that if Jesus could walk on water, so could he. Christ had not only instructed Peter that through faith he could perform miracles, but he had also commanded Peter to perform miracles in His name. Peter, seeing the miracle of walking on water, exercised his faith to perform this miracle also. A key to understanding this story is the phrase, 'when Peter was come down out of the ship, he walked on the water.'[88]

"Peter walked on water. It's not surprising that Jesus walked on water. He is God. He fed five thousand with two fish and five loaves of bread. He cast out devils, raised the dead, and He healed the sick. I believe it's much easier to believe that Christ can perform such miracles than it is to believe that you can perform such miracles in His name. The most amazing part of the story is that Peter, a mere man, walked on water."

Naniwaiwai continued, "I've pondered on why Jesus would have answered, 'Come,' in response to Peter's request to walk on the water. What was the purpose? The impression that came to me in answer to this question was that Jesus was showing Peter, the other disciples in the boat, and each of us who reads the New Testament today, that with faith in Christ, we can each do the mighty miracles that Christ performed. Reading about Peter walking on water should increase our faith to perform miracles in the name of the Lord. If we believe in Christ, signs and miracles will occur."

Naniwaiwai turned to another passage of scripture and read, "'And these signs shall follow them that believe; In my name shall they cast out devils; they shall speak with new tongues; they shall take up serpents; and if they drink any deadly thing, it shall not hurt them: they shall lay hands on the sick, and they shall recover.'[89]

"Jesus is speaking to you when he says, 'If you can believe, all things are possible.'[90] You should strive to follow the example of the disciple Stephen, who 'full of faith and power did great wonders and miracles among the people.'[91]

Listening to her made me want to fulfill the commission of my Savior to perform miracles in His name.

As I sat pondering on Naniwaiwai's words, she turned the pages of her Bible and began speaking again. "Elder Taylor, the gospel of John provides another account of Jesus walking on the water following the feeding of the five thousand and there is an interesting detail in this account that often goes unnoticed."

She stopped turning the pages and began to read, "'His disciples went down to the sea, got into the boat, and went over the sea toward Capernaum. And it was already dark, and Jesus had not come to them. Then the sea arose because a great wind was blowing. So when they had rowed about three or four miles, they saw Jesus walking on the sea and drawing near the boat; and they were afraid. But He said to them, 'It is I; do not be afraid.' Then they willingly received Him into the boat, and immediately the boat was at the land where they were going.'[92]

"The distance they were traveling across the Sea of Galilee to Capernaum was between six and seven miles. The account says they had traveled three to four miles when Jesus entered the boat. They still had three to four miles to travel before they arrived in Capernaum and yet the scriptures record that when Jesus entered the boat, 'immediately the boat was at the land where they were going.'[93] This miracle is often overlooked since we focus on the miracle of walking on the water. Jesus moved a boat three miles in an instant. With faith in His name, you can do the same."

There was a moment of silence. I pondered on the wisdom and insights Naniwaiwai had shared. I was surprised that despite my many readings of the New Testament, I had never noticed this miracle of Jesus transporting the boat. I offered a silent prayer of thanks for the opportunity to sit at the feet and be taught by a mighty disciple of the Lord Jesus Christ.

Naniwaiwai broke the silence. "Elder Taylor, you can touch the temple now if you would like."

I rose to my feet and moved toward the temple. I had the impression that I should walk around the building before touching it, so I slowly circled around the entire edifice. I approached one of the large rocks in the wall of the temple and placed my hand on it. As I put my hand on the temple, I asked the rock for its thoughts, believing the rock would speak to me. Immediately, my mind was filled with the words, "It is an honor and a privilege to be a part of the house of the Lord."

I kept my hand on the temple and followed the impression to walk around the temple while running my hand along its walls. I held my right hand on the temple and walked clockwise around the structure, rubbing my fingers against the stones of the building. I felt it was important to maintain contact with the temple for the complete rotation, overlapping where I had begun.

I finished a complete rotation around the temple but had the impression to repeat the same exercise with my left hand. I placed my left hand on the temple and without breaking contact with the building, began walking counterclockwise around the temple, my fingers again running along the stones of the structure until I had overlapped where I had begun.

I found a place to sit where I was centered with the temple's outside walls, with half of the temple on my right and half of the temple on my left. As I sat in stillness and silence, I was given the words, "Consecrate and sanctify yourself for tomorrow the LORD will do great wonders among you."[94]

After hearing these words, I asked the Lord for forgiveness so that I could become a sanctified and clean vessel—a conduit for His power, His wonders, and His blessings. The Spirit brought the plaque behind the pulpit in Keōmoku Church on Lanaʻi into my mind. I saw the word "*Hoolaaia*" and remembered how the Keōmoku Church was sanctified, dedicated, and consecrated to the Lord. I had the thought that this mountain temple is a house of the Lord—sanctified, consecrated, and dedicated to the Lord and His purposes. My fingers tingled from the texture of the stone rubbing against them. I had the impression that as I ran my hands across this holy edifice that some of the temple's *mana* and consecration had gone from the building into my hands.

I had the impression that I should consecrate my hands to God and the Lord Jesus Christ. Following the impression, I began to pray. "Holy Father, I consecrate my hands to do Thy work and the work of thy Beloved Son. Bless me to use my hands to lift, bless, heal, and build Thy kingdom. In the holy and sacred name of Jesus

Christ, Amen." As I concluded my prayer, tears streamed down my cheeks as the Spirit filled my hands and my body. My hands were now sanctified and consecrated, prepared to do great wonders in the name of the Lord.

I sat in silence until I felt a hand on my shoulder. "It's time to head down the mountain if we want to get home before dark," Manu said.

He helped me to my feet and we walked over to Naniwaiwai to express our thanks.

I bowed slightly as I stood in front of her, feeling like it was the right thing to do to show my respect. "Naniwaiwai," I said, "thank you for sharing with me the gifts of faith, hope, and charity. Thank you for helping me believe."

"Thank you for being prepared to learn and willing to receive, Elder Taylor," she gently replied.

After Manu expressed his gratitude and respect to Naniwaiwai and we both expressed our thanks and respect to the four *pueo* on each corner of the temple, we began our journey down the mountain. One of the *pueo* flew ahead of us, guiding us back to Naniwaiwai's home. While neither Manu nor I spoke about how Naniwaiwai would return home, we both knew she would arrive at her house long before we did.

CHAPTER 14
MANA

"Mana is the spiritual energy that we are all born with. God has put this energy in the earth and the heavens."

- Kupuna Alex Pua'a

As we made our way through the trees and brush, Manu asked, "Do you mind if I ask what you were you doing when you were walking around the temple rubbing your hands along the stone?"

I didn't know how to convey my experience using words, so I simply said, "I was sanctifying and consecrating my hands to both God and the Lord Jesus Christ." I attempted to articulate to Manu the thoughts, impressions, directions, and words I was given by the Spirit during my time at the temple.

After I finished sharing, Manu was silent for a time before speaking. "Elder Taylor, I was filled with the Spirit as you told of your experience. I believe God revealed to you an ancient protocol for disciples of the Lord Jesus Christ to sanctify and consecrate their hands to God and Christ. You mentioned that you felt that some of the temple's *mana* was transferred into your hands. Correct?"

"Yes," I replied.

"As you know, *mana* is spiritual power. It's God's power, and it can be stored in physical objects. When the stones for the temple were moved to the top of the mountain by the miracle of God's power, a portion of the power used to move these stones was stored inside them. Then, when the completed temple was dedicated and consecrated by our *kūpuna*, the stones were sanctified and consecrated by God's power, and more power was garnered in these stones. In addition, since this sacred *heiau* is a house of the Lord, whenever God visited this temple, His light, truth, and power radiated from Him and more of His power was accumulated in those stones.

"I hadn't ever really considered the idea of God's power being able to be stored in objects, but it makes a lot of sense," I said.

"It does make sense, doesn't it, Elder Taylor? Did you know that you can find many examples in the scriptures and in church history of *mana* being stored in objects?"

For a moment my mind raced through accounts in the scriptures that Manu might be referring to, but I couldn't think of any. Manu had my complete attention.

"Elder Taylor, I think one of the most well-known examples of *mana* being stored in an object is the robe of Jesus Christ. As Jesus walked through throngs of people, a woman who had been sick for twelve years pushed through the crowd, hoping that if she could simply touch His robe she would be healed. When she touched the hem of the Savior's robe, she was immediately healed.[95]

"Her experience wasn't an isolated instance. Many were healed by touching the robe of Jesus. These healings resulted in groups pressing upon Him, hoping to touch His robe and be healed. Matthew, Mark, and Luke each record accounts of this occurring."

We paused for a moment and Manu retrieved his book of notes from his backpack. He thumbed through the pages until he found what he was looking for and began reading Mark 6:56, "'And whithersoever he entered, into villages, or cities, or country, they laid the sick in the streets, and besought him that they might touch if it were but the border of his garment: and as many as touched him were made whole.'"[96] Manu continued, "Mark 3:10 reads, 'He had healed many, so that those with diseases were pushing forward to touch him.'[97] Luke 6:19 records a similar account, 'The whole multitude sought to touch him: for there went power out of him, and healed them all.'[98] And Matthew 14:35-36 reads, 'When the people recognized Jesus, the news of his arrival spread quickly throughout the whole area, and soon people were bringing all their sick to be healed. They begged him to let the sick touch at least the fringe of his robe, and all who touched him were healed.'"[99]

As Manu finished reading these passages, I felt completely dumbfounded. The words and their meaning seemed clear as Manu read them to me and yet, I had never noticed these verses before. I had read the New Testament more times than I could count. How had I never contemplated on these things?

Manu continued, "Holders of the Holy Melchizedek priesthood carry a substance that possesses great healing power. Jesus went to the Garden of Gethsemane at the base of the Mount of Olives to perform the first component of the Atonement. The word Gethsemane comes from two Hebrew roots: 'gath' meaning 'press,' and 'shemen' meaning 'olive oil.' Olives were pressed under the weight of great stone wheels that would squeeze oil from them. Likewise, in the Garden of Gethsemane, Jesus was literally pressed under the weight of the sins, pains, and sicknesses of the world. This weight caused Jesus to fall upon His face as He was pressed into the ground.[100] This press upon the Savior of the world caused His precious blood to drip from every pore of His body."[101]

Manu's voice slowed, trembling with emotion as he spoke of the sacred events that took place in the garden.

"When olive oil is consecrated for the healing of the sick, it becomes the healing blood of the Lord Jesus Christ. Thus, each time you anoint an individual with consecrated oil olive, that person is touched with Christ's sacred and holy blood and by faith, they can be healed through His blood. As holders of God's priesthood, we should understand what we're doing when we perform this sacred ordinance. We're literally touching a person with the sacred and powerful blood of the Lord Jesus—blood that contains His healing power.

"Regrettably, if we're not careful, it's possible for us as priesthood holders to simply go through the procedure of anointing and sealing without accessing Christ's healing power. The Apostle Paul described this best when he said, 'Having a form of godliness, but denying the power thereof.'[102] When ordinances are performed with the power of Christ's healing blood, multitudes will press upon the elders of the church, pleading to be touched by the healing blood of the Lord Jesus Christ."

"Your words reminded me of President Nelson's comments in Priesthood session." I opened the conference talk on my phone and read the quote brought to my remembrance. "'Too many of our brothers and sisters do not grasp the privileges that could be theirs. Let me give you some specific examples. Not long ago, I attended a sacrament meeting in which a new baby was to be given a name and a father's blessing. The young father held his precious infant in his arms, gave her a name, and then offered a beautiful prayer. But he did not give that child a blessing. That sweet baby girl got a name but no blessing! That dear elder did not know the difference between a prayer and a priesthood blessing. With his priesthood authority and power, he could have blessed his infant, but he did not. I thought, 'What a missed opportunity!' Let me cite some other examples. We know of brethren who set sisters apart as Primary, Young Women, or Relief Society leaders and teachers but fail to bless them—to bless them with the power to fulfill their callings. They give only admonitions and instructions. We see a worthy father who fails to give his wife and his children priesthood blessings when that is exactly what they need. Priesthood power has been restored to this earth, and yet far too many brothers and sisters go through terrible trials in life without ever receiving a true priesthood blessing. What a tragedy!'"[103]

Manu nodded his head. "It is a tragedy. The challenge of priesthood holders learning to use the power of the priesthood isn't unique to our day, Elder Taylor. The New Testament records accounts of the apostles blessing the sick but failing to heal them.[104] These same individuals later went to the Savior and were healed. The apostles had to be taught by the Savior how to use the power of His priesthood to heal as He did.

"There were similar problems in the early restored church.

While in Nauvoo, Joseph Smith rebuked elders 'who would continue to lay hands on the sick...without the power to heal them.' Joseph warned, 'It's time that such things ended. Let the Elders either obtain the power of God to heal the sick or let them cease to minister the forms without the power.'[105]

"Wilford Woodruff recorded what he called 'The Day of Miracles' when the power of God rested mightily upon Joseph Smith. Like Jesus in His day, Joseph healed all the sick around him. In the beginning years, Nauvoo was a swampy, unhealthy place. Many were bedridden with serious illnesses. Joseph went among the sick that were lying on the bank of the river and in a loud voice commanded them in the name of Jesus Christ to rise and be made whole, and they were all healed. After Joseph had healed all on the east side of the river that were sick, he and his companions crossed the Mississippi River in a ferryboat to the west side, to Montrose. The first house they went into was President Brigham Young's. He was sick on his bed at the time. The Prophet went into his house and healed him, and they all came out together.

"As they passed Wilford Woodruff's house, they called for Wilford to join them and they entered Brother Fordham's house. Joseph walked up to Brother Fordham and took him by the right hand. Brother Fordham's eyes were glazed. He was speechless and unconscious. After taking his hand, Joseph looked down into the dying man's face and said: 'Elijah, do you not know me?' With a low whisper Brother Fordham answered, 'Yes.' The Prophet then said: 'Do you have the faith to be healed?' The answer, which was a little plainer than before, was: 'I'm afraid it's too late; if you had come sooner, I think I might have been healed.' He had the appearance of a man waking from the sleep of death. Joseph then said: 'Do you believe that Jesus is the Christ?' 'I do, Brother Joseph,' was the response. Then the Prophet of God spoke with a loud voice, as in the majesty of Jehovah: 'Elijah, I command you, in the name of Jesus of Nazareth, to arise and be made whole.' The words of the Prophet were not like the words of man, but like the voice of God. Elijah Fordham leaped from his bed like a man raised from the dead. A healthy color came to his face, and life was manifested in every act. He called for his clothes and put them on. He asked for a bowl of bread and milk, and ate it. He then put on his hat and followed them into the street to visit others who were sick.

"They next went to the home of Joseph B. Noble, who was very sick. When they entered the house, Brother Joseph took Brother Noble by the hand and commanded him in the name of Jesus Christ to arise and be made whole. Brother Noble arose and was healed immediately. They went from Brother Noble's home to the bank of the river, to return home.

"While waiting for the ferryboat, a man who wasn't a member of the church came to Joseph. He had heard of the miracles that had been performed and asked Joseph if he would heal his five-month-old twins who were sick unto death. Joseph turned to Wilford Woodruff and said, 'You go with the man and heal his children.' Joseph took a red silk handkerchief out of his pocket, gave it to Wilford, and told him to wipe the infants' faces with the handkerchief when he administered to them, and that they would be healed. Joseph told Wilford, 'As long as you will keep that handkerchief, it shall remain a league between you and me.' Wilford Woodruff went with the man, did as the Prophet commanded him, and the children were healed.[106]

"This handkerchief is on display at the Church History Museum in Salt Lake City and is a treasure worth more than gold. To some it seems strange that Joseph Smith would give Wilford Woodruff a handkerchief to use as a part of the healing, but for those who understand *mana* and the importance of connections, it's not strange. In fact, the New Testament records the apostles using handkerchiefs in a similar manner."

Manu flipped through his book of notes and said, "Acts 19:11-12 reads, 'God did extraordinary miracles through Paul, so that even handkerchiefs and aprons that had touched him were taken to the sick, and their illnesses were cured, and the evil spirits left them.'[107]

"Just as the *mana*-filled handkerchief provided Wilford Woodruff a connection to the Prophet Joseph Smith and the faith to heal, the consecrated olive oil connects you and those you bless to Jesus Christ and His healing blood, the source of all power and healing."

We sat in silence for a moment and I tried to absorb what I was being taught. Manu stood from our resting spot. The *pueo* continued to guide us down the mountain staying twenty to thirty yards ahead of us. The trip down was definitely much easier than the climb up. It was a joy to be in the sacred *'āina* of Hālawa Valley and be renewed by her spirit, beauty, energy, and Aloha.

As we arrived back at Naniwaiwai's home, she greeted us with her usual hug, kiss, and warm Aloha.

"Come in. Come in. I thought you would be extra hungry after a long day of hiking, so I have a feast prepared for you."

"That's good because I'm starving!" I exclaimed. The meal was amazing, and I found myself eating several plates of food. In between bites, I managed to say, "Naniwaiwai, this food is delicious. What's your secret?"

"Elder Taylor, I often sing and dance while I cook to infuse the food with joy, love, and power. I believe that you should prepare food to feed both the body and the spirit. I've found that food prepared with Aloha tastes better."

"I suppose that shouldn't surprise me, Naniwaiwai," I replied. "Aloha makes everything better."

"Aloha does make everything better," boomed Manu. "It's the secret ingredient to a joyful life!"

Following dinner, Manu and I cleaned the kitchen while Naniwaiwai rested on the *lanai*. As we cleaned, we heard the sweet sounds of the *'ukulele* and the beautiful melodies of Naniwaiwai's voice.

Once we finished cleaning, we joined Naniwaiwai on the *lanai*, and she and Manu took turns playing the *'ukulele*. We sang, danced, laughed, and played. There was no need for a television, an iPad, a cell phone or an Xbox. We had something far more rewarding—an *'ukulele* and the gifts of song, dance, and friendship.

Saturday's long day of hiking left me sore the next morning. Since it was the Sabbath, I dressed for church, putting on my suit and tie, and began studying my scriptures as I waited for Manu and Naniwaiwai. Naniwaiwai had informed us that the only church building on the island was located an hour's drive from her home.

The building was shared by two wards. The Hoolehua Ward was attended by those who lived on the west half of the island, while the Kaunakakai Ward was attended by those who lived on the east half of the island.

I heard light, joyful footsteps coming down the hallway and looked up to see Naniwaiwai emerging in a bright, beautiful floral dress. She looked me in the eyes and greeted me with, "*Pehea kou piko?*"

I paused for a moment, pondering on the significance of her question and answered with the Hawaiian word for good, "*Maikaʻi.*"

Naniwaiwai sat on the living room floor and began meditating. Manu entered the room a few minutes later, sat on the couch, and began reading his scriptures.

The house remained silent as Manu and I studied and Naniwaiwai meditated. Eventually, Naniwaiwai rose to her feet and extended a hand to both Manu and me. As the three of us formed a circle, Naniwaiwai began to chant, followed by Manu offering a chant. At the conclusion of Manu's chant, I began reciting the chant I had learned the day before.

After finishing my chant, we released hands and greeted each other with a *honi*. As Naniwaiwai stepped back from greeting Manu, she said, "Manu, I see you have several holes in your suit jacket."

"Why yes, Naniwaiwai, I do," Manu replied, pointing to a worn area at the elbow.

"Manu, if you will please give me your jacket, I would love to repair those holes on our drive to church."

"I appreciate your generous offer, Naniwaiwai, but that isn't necessary," Manu replied.

"It may not be necessary, Manu," Naniwaiwai replied with a kind smile, "but it would bring me great joy to repair it. Please hand me your coat."

"You better give her your jacket, Manu." I laughed as we both realized we were no match for Naniwaiwai's determination or generosity.

"I think you're right, Elder Taylor. I think you're right," Manu replied with a chuckle.

Manu removed his jacket while Naniwaiwai retrieved a sewing kit, and we made our way to the car. It was clear that Manu's suit was extremely old, and I was curious as to why he hadn't purchased a new one yet. "Manu, isn't it time for a new suit?" I asked.

Smiling, Manu said, "Most people would have replaced this suit a long time ago, but it's filled with so much *mana* that I don't want to part with it."

"What do you mean?"

Manu answered, "I've participated in dozens of priesthood blessings and ordinances while wearing this suit. I've seen miracles of healing. I've seen miracles of revelation. I've seen miracles of visions. I've felt the hand of the Lord touching and healing. Just as *mana* was stored in the robe of Jesus and in the handkerchief of Joseph Smith, a portion of the power and spirit that flows during blessings is stored in this suit. When I put on this suit, I can feel the *mana* from these blessing and miracles, and it builds my faith."

"The Spirit has brought a story to my mind," I responded. "My family and I are friends with President Monson's son, Clark, and his wife Patty and their two children, Paul and Sally. We were neighbors when we lived in Provo, Utah. We served together in various callings in the ward and our children played together. President Monson would attend our ward to watch his grandchildren in the primary program. I remember on one of President Monson's visits, he greeted me and my family with a handshake as he came up the aisle on his way to the podium. I noticed a large hole in the sleeve of his suit coat as he shook my hand. I thought it odd that President Monson was wearing a suit with holes in it. I now think that President Monson may have worn a suit with holes for the same reason you do."

Manu smiled and replied, "When you recognize the *mana* that's stored in the fibers of your suit, it makes it very difficult to get a new suit."

"A few years ago, I read a biography on President Spencer W. Kimball written by his son, Ed. In the book, a story is shared about President Kimball wearing shoes filled with holes. A church leader mentioned this fact to President Kimball's assistant one day. His assistant replied, 'Has he got that pair on again? I've taken that pair away from him and hidden them a dozen times! He's got all kinds of new shoes, but he loves that old pair.' Another story was shared of a check for $40 arriving at church headquarters for President Kimball to buy a new pair of shoes. The check was sent shortly after President Kimball had attended a meeting at the Rose Bowl. A man who had viewed the proceedings through binoculars observed that President Kimball's shoes contained serious wear and holes. When President Kimball was told of the money for a new pair of shoes, he laughed and told his assistant to put the money in the missionary fund."[108]

Manu and Naniwaiwai both laughed. "That's a wonderful story, Elder Taylor," Naniwaiwai said.

Manu replied, "I hadn't heard the story about President Kimball's shoes, but I can understand why he would prefer the old pair. His shoes would have contained years of *mana*."

We drove in silence for a time, enjoying the peace and beauty of the south side of Moloka'i with its lush green mountains to our right and the vast blue ocean to our left.

Naniwaiwai spoke, breaking the silence. "Manu, I've completed the repair of your suit. It will be good for many more years."

"*Mahalo*," Manu replied, speaking slowly.

At first, I wasn't sure if it was Manu's voice or the word itself, but a warmth spread through the car as the word "*Mahalo*" was spoken. It filled the space like water moves through any opening it finds, spreading until it seemed as if it always belonged there.

Naniwaiwai's face radiated the same Spirit. Her "Aloha, brother" told me I wasn't the only one who felt it. Her words added to the power until I thought the Spirit might burst out the windows.

"I've heard the word *mahalo* many times, but this time it felt different," I said.

"*Mahalo* is a word with great spiritual power," Manu replied. "It's to be spoken with breath, life, love, and reverence. It should come more from the heart and soul than from the mouth and tongue. *Mahalo* is often translated to English as 'thank you,' but *mahalo* is much more than a word of thanks. *Mahalo* is undefinable with words alone. To be fully understood, it must be experienced. *Mahalo* is a single-word prayer and blessing. It's an expression of love and gratitude. *Mahalo* is as important as Aloha and expresses sacred and spiritual truths. Both words contain the root word '*ha*," which represents God and His gift of breath. Both words also contain the root word '*alo*' which means 'presence.' *Mahalo* begins with the root word '*ma*' which means 'because of.' Looking at the root words of *mahalo*, a better translation to English would be, 'Because of God's presence.' *Mahalo* is an expression of Divine favor. It's a word used to express admiration, praise, and esteem to God."

"*Mahalo*, Manu. That was beautiful," Naniwaiwai said. "Elder Taylor, Manu has done a superb job of describing *mahalo* as well as one possibly can using words. However, as you just experienced, you will learn the most about *mahalo* through your feelings. You felt reverence, love, gratitude, power, spirit, and humility. That's *mahalo*. *Mahalo* isn't something you say. *Mahalo* is something you are. *Mahalo* isn't a word to speak, but a way to live. Your bowl, your *na'au*, your bowels, should be full of gratitude. For *mahalo* to truly be spoken, your bowl must be full of light, love, and gratitude."

Manu nodded in agreement and spoke, "My grandfather shared with me a phrase I have repeated often. 'When you exhale gratitude, you inhale love and joy.'"

I didn't want our conversation to end, but we had arrived at Kaunakakai, and I could see the church building ahead on the right. After finding a place to park, Manu opened Naniwaiwai's door for her and helped her from the car. Naniwaiwai handed Manu his suit jacket and he slipped it on.

"I can feel your love in my jacket, Naniwaiwai," Manu said.

Smiling, Naniwaiwai replied, "Yes, Manu, your suit is now filled with my touch of Aloha. Repairing a suit with your hands may not be the most efficient method but it's the most effective. It's an act of Aloha. The sharing of Aloha is of far greater value than the time and money saved having it done by a machine or at a shop. The simple act of repairing a suit with your hands creates connection."

Manu and Naniwaiwai placed their foreheads together and shared breath. Manu breathed the word, "*Mahalo*."

"Aloha," Naniwaiwai replied.

Manu answered, "Aloha."

Naniwaiwai again replied, "Aloha."

They parted foreheads and Manu took Naniwaiwai by the arm to escort her into the building.

As we walked toward the church, I commented, "I could feel the love increase as you each spoke."

Naniwaiwai smiled. "That's one of the magical characteristics of Aloha, Elder Taylor. When it's shared, it grows."

I walked ahead of them to open the doors, but before I reached the doors, a group of people excitedly came out of the building. We were each greeted with hugs and kisses. Following the greetings, the group took turns placing lei around our necks. It was an outpouring of love, hospitality, friendship, and joy that brought tears to my eyes.

We were escorted into the foyer and immediately began talking story. Many were excited to meet the Elder Taylor and Manu they had read about in *The Way of Aloha: Lanaʻi*. A few minutes before the sacrament meeting was scheduled to start, we were directed to seats that had been reserved for us. I looked at the program as we sat in the quiet chapel waiting for the meeting to start. On the front of the program was a large church logo and a picture of Jesus Christ as the Good Shepherd.

THE CHURCH OF
JESUS CHRIST
OF LATTER-DAY SAINTS

As I looked at the logo, I received the impression that I should emphasize the Lord Jesus Christ in all I do. I should follow the example of my brothers and sisters in the Book of Mormon who said, "We talk of Christ, we rejoice in Christ, we preach of Christ, we prophesy of Christ, and we write according to our prophecies, that our children may know to what source they may look for a remission of their sins."[109]

The Spirit taught me that just as the focus of the Church logo is Jesus Christ, so the focus of *The Way of Aloha* book series should be the Lord Jesus Christ. All the principles and stories that are shared are to bring people to Christ and provide a greater understanding of Him, His Gospel, and His grace. Our world is in need of hope and friendship, and hope and friendship are found in the Lord Jesus Christ.

The Way of Aloha books are to be a catalyst for readers to be touched by the Savior. Readers need to feel Christ's touch of peace, love, joy, healing, friendship, and forgiveness. They need to see themselves as Christ sees them because when you see yourself as Christ sees you, you're filled with a perfect brightness of hope. The principles of Aloha and the principles of Christ are the same.

I pulled a pen from my suit coat and wrote my impressions down on the program. As I was writing my notes, Bishop Hao walked to the podium and opened the meeting with a warm Aloha. "Aloha," the congregation responded in unison.

The experience I had just had with Manu and Naniwaiwai exchanging Aloha helped me understand the significance of each person sharing Aloha as they took the podium and for the audience to respond in return with Aloha. It was a way to share Aloha and for it to grow.

It happened to be the first Sunday of the month, so I experienced the power of Aloha in even greater abundance as members of the congregation rose to bear their testimonies. As each person stood at the podium, they began with "Aloha" followed by a loud "Aloha" echoing from the congregation. The Spirit and love in the room increased with each Aloha and testimony of the Lord. The word Aloha is much more than a greeting. Saying Aloha is a way to share your love of the Lord Jesus Christ, praise His Holy name, and share His perfect love.

The closing hymn was "Israel, Israel, God Is Calling," a song that held a special place in my heart since my brothers and I sang this song in Hawaiian at my missionary homecoming. As we sang, tears filled my eyes as I was overcome by the spirit, power, and message of this magnificent hymn.

Following the closing prayer, we were again surrounded by our friends, talking story until it was time for Sunday school. During Sunday school, I noticed that nearly everyone had their printed scriptures in hand. It didn't matter if they were old or young. They all had printed scriptures.

I waited until after Sunday school to ask Manu, "I noticed that most of the members were using printed scriptures instead of tablets or smart phones. Do you have smart phones on Moloka'i?"

Manu laughed, "Of course, we have smartphones, but those who are wise don't use them for scripture study. While digital scriptures have many wonderful uses and advantages, there are also many disadvantages. Just as I don't want to buy a new suit because it now has an accumulation of *mana*, I also don't want to buy a new set of scriptures because my scriptures contain an accumulation of *mana*. As you read from the pages of your scriptures and are filled with the Spirit, a portion of that spirit is stored in the pages. This spirit and power builds day after day and year after year. Your scriptures become a reservoir of spiritual strength and *mana* that can be felt when you open the book. It's much harder for *mana* to be stored and retained in a digital device. Furthermore, *mana* that's stored in a digital device is frequently lost since smartphones and tablets become obsolete and are replaced. The printed scriptures can be kept for a lifetime, storing decades of spirit, power, and experience."

Manu continued, "Another downfall of digital devices is that you use them to check your email, make phone calls, work, play games and coordinate your calendar. The device can be infused with negative energy from these other uses and the positive spirit and *mana* of scripture study can be eliminated or diluted. The printed scriptures' *mana* can be kept pure and undiluted more easily as printed scriptures are only used for study and only contain the Word of God.

It's important to utilize and study the printed scriptures even though, at times, it's easier and more convenient to use digital scriptures."

I stood in silence for a few moments, knowing that how I viewed and used digital and printed scriptures would never be the same. "*Mahalo*, Manu." I finally said. "I see the wisdom in what you've taught. My eyes have been opened, and I understand things in a way I hadn't before. *Mahalo*."

CHAPTER 15

KAPUAIWA ROYAL COCONUT GROVE

"For the Lamb…shall feed them, and shall lead them unto living fountains of waters: and God shall wipe away all tears from their eyes."

- Revelation 7:17, King James Version

I still had much to contemplate after the services were over, but Manu had more in store for me. Naniwaiwai stayed behind to visit. Manu and I walked through the church parking lot and across the street, taking in the sunshine of the glorious Hawaiian Sabbath.

Manu turned to face the LDS church and pointed to the other churches that lined the street. "This is called church row. Sunday morning is the busiest you will see the streets of Moloka'i."

"This is my kind of busy," I said, smiling. Although there were cars coming and going from the churches, a quiet and relaxed feeling permeated the area. We turned to look at the grove of coconut trees that sat between the tidy row of churches and the ocean.

"These trees were planted in 1863 by King Kamehameha V and is called the Kapuaiwa Royal Coconut Grove," Manu said.

Coconut trees towered over the sand, reaching into the clear, blue sky. "How many trees are in the grove?" I asked.

"There are about a thousand trees on ten acres," Manu answered. "A fence was recently placed around the grove to protect this sacred place. Some locals and tourists don't understand the history and importance so, at times, the grove hasn't been treated with proper respect. Some locals and tourists don't understand the need to *pule* (pray) and ask permission before entering. The fence was recently constructed to protect this culturally and historically rich place from being misused."

"Are we allowed to enter the grove?" I asked.

"If we're granted permission, yes."

We walked down the road bordering the west side of the coconut grove, walking toward the ocean. There was a group of local young men hanging out on the side of the road around their truck. As we approached the young men, Manu greeted them with, "Howzit, braddahs?" ("Howzit, braddah?" is a common local greeting.)

Manu clasped each of their hands, gave them half-hugs, and asked them about their families. Several connections were made, with one of the young men exclaiming, "Wez cuzins, braddah!"

"Yeah, wez cuzins," Manu answered.

After a few minutes of talking story, Manu asked, "What do you know about this coconut grove?"

The young men shrugged their shoulders and Manu said, "Braddahs, why don't you join us in the grove."

There was always much more to Manu's voice than words. A love, concern, joy, and excitement flowed with his invitation. The young men shrugged, looked at each other, and one of the young men announced, "Why not, cuz."

Our group walked to the end of the road. The fence surrounding the grove ended before the beach. Manu stopped at the end of the fence and said, "This place is *wahi pana* (sacred). Before we enter the grove, we must *pule* (pray) and ask permission to enter."

Manu began taking deep breaths and exhaling with, "*Haaaaaaaaa*." The young men and I followed Manu's lead. Soon, we were all breathing in unison.

Manu stopped and said, "Now, please take a moment in silence to ask God, your ancestors, and the keepers of this place for permission to enter."

Minutes went by before Manu asked the young men, "How do you feel?"

"Chicken skin, braddah," one young man answered.

"Yeah, chicken skin," the other young men replied.

I had learned as a missionary that Hawaiians often described feeling the Spirit or feeling the presence of their ancestors with the words "chicken skin."

"How about you, Elder Taylor?" Manu asked.

"Yes. Chicken skin," I answered with a smile.

"Well, it sounds like we've all received permission to enter. Please remember to be reverent, humble, and compassionate while we're in the grove. It's *hewa* (wrong) to speak or act disrespectfully in a place of *wahi pana*. Before we enter, we should offer thanks."

Manu began to chant:

Uhola ʻia ka makaloa lā

Pū ʻai i ke Aloha ā

Kū kaʻi ʻia ka hā loa lā

Pāwehi mai nā lehua
Mai ka hoʻokuʻi a ka hālāwai lā
Mahalo e Nā Akua
Mahalo e nā kūpuna lā, ʻeā
Mahalo me ke Aloha lā
Mahalo me ke Aloha lā

The chant penetrated my soul, and I was filled with love, thanks, and joy. After discreetly wiping tears from his eyes, one of the young men asked, "Will you teach me this chant?"

Smiling, Manu answered, "Of course."

Manu, a master teacher, radiated excitement at having a student ask to be taught. "This chant is called 'Oli Mahalo,'" Manu said.

Manu chanted one line of the *oli* while the rest of us repeated the words.

"Very good. Very good," Manu said, smiling. "Let's try it one more time."

Manu again chanted a line of the *oli* while we echoed the words.

As we completed our second attempt, one of the young men asked, "What does the chant mean?"

"I'm assuming you recognized many of the words we spoke, correct?" Manu asked. The young men nodded in agreement. "I'll do my best to express the meaning of the *oli* in English. However, Hawaiian doesn't translate easily, so it will be difficult to fully capture the full spirit and meaning of this *oli* in English. It would mean something along these lines:

My heart is open
Let us gather to share our love and life

Let this place be honored, respected, and beatified now and forever

Admiration, praise, and gratitude to God

Admiration, praise, and gratitude to our beloved ancestors

Admiration, praise, gratitude, and love to all who are present, both seen and unseen

After a moment of silence, Manu slipped the shoes and socks from his feet and crossed into the coconut grove. The young men removed their flip-flops, and I removed my shoes and socks. We followed Manu as he walked along the beach, the trees to our left and the ocean to our right.

The feel of sand on my feet and between my toes was refreshing. I could feel a connection to the ʻāina and the keepers of this sacred place. Manu turned into the grove and walked toward the center. The young men and I followed. As we walked into the grove, a small stream seemed to appear out of nowhere. We soon came to the source of the stream—a fresh water spring. The clear turquoise water stood out against the vibrant green foliage.

We formed a circle around the spring, and Manu began to teach us. "This is a sacred spring that has flowed for many years. King Kamehameha V planted one thousand coconut trees to represent one thousand warriors who were assigned to protect this land and this spring."

Manu looked up to the top of the trees and asked, "Can you see the warriors? Can you see your ancestors caring for and protecting this place?"

As Manu said these words, gusts of wind rushed through the trees, a manifestation of the unseen who were with us. As we looked up and viewed the hundreds of sky-piercing palms rustling and swaying in the wind, I was infused with hope, love, and goodness and felt as if the trees were embracing me in a hug.

Pointing to a tree that rose above the rest, Manu said, "This tree represents the *Kahu* (the keeper) of this place. This tree was recently recognized as the largest known Palm Coconut in the country and was declared a Champion Tree by the nonprofit organization called American Forests.[110] The *Kahu* of Kapuaiwa Grove is one-hundred-and-three feet tall. Many drive past and only see a group of coconut trees, but those who know the story see an army of a thousand warriors protecting this fountain of living water."

I was struck by the words "living water" and asked Manu, "What do you mean by living water?"

"Elder Taylor, what's the difference between well water and spring water?"

I thought for a moment and replied, "Well water is pulled from deep in the ground and spring water flows freely above the ground."

"That's right, Elder Taylor," Manu replied. "A spring is a powerful symbol of the Lord Jesus Christ. At the time these trees were planted, the Kingdom of Hawai'i was one of the greatest Christian nations on the earth. Many recognized Jesus Christ as the God of light and peace they had worshiped and followed before the *kapu* system. In the Bible, we find profound truths taught by the Savior using the symbols of both a well and a spring. Christ taught, 'My people have done two evils: They have turned away from Me, the spring of living water. And they have dug their own wells, which are broken wells that cannot hold water.'[111]

"The Lord is teaching us a parable about His grace. In this parable, Jesus isn't referring to just any people. Jesus says, 'My people.' Jesus is speaking to His followers, to members of His church. Jesus offers the gift of living water, the gifts of life, forgiveness, and salvation, and yet, His people turn away from Him to dig their own wells. Instead of receiving from the spring of living water by receiving His grace and His forgiveness, His people seek to dig their own wells.

"Instead of receiving of the living water which he freely gives, they turn away from the spring to dig deep into the ground. Instead of receiving the gift of grace springing forth, they focus on their works in an attempt to produce their own water. They seek to quench their thirst for life, forgiveness and salvation with their own works, but the wells they dig produce no water. They may dig harder, faster, and deeper but they will never find living water in their works. The wells of works are dry.

Manu continued, "Grace isn't earned with the work of a shovel. Grace is a gift received with a broken heart and a contrite spirit. We should not seek a man-made well but a God-given spring. Forgiveness, salvation, and eternal life are not rewards for digging a well, but freely given gifts we must receive.

"Jesus is the spring of living water—the only spring that will quench your thirst for forgiveness, salvation, and eternal life. Those who thirst for the Son of Righteous[112] will be filled[113] with living water. You should put down your shovel of salvation by works and cry aloud saying, 'Lord, I thirst.'[114] The New Testament records seven statements of Christ from the cross. When Jesus said on the cross, 'I thirst,' they gave him vinegar. When you say, 'Lord, I thirst,' He gives you living water.

"The Lord declares, 'If any man thirst, let him come unto me, and drink…[115] Whoever drinks the water I give them will never thirst. Indeed, the water I give them will become in them a spring of water welling up to eternal life.'"[116]

It began to rain lightly as Manu taught us about living water. As the rain stopped, Manu pointed and said, "Look." As we gazed in the direction he was pointing, we saw a rainbow forming over the ocean. We walked the short distance to the beach to obtain a clearer view. The rainbow began to form to our left, just above the ocean, and expanded to the right. Within a few moments, the whole rainbow came into view. It was an immense rainbow with vibrant color. The top of the arch was ahead of us and the ends of the rainbow were to our left and to our right, stopping at the surface of the ocean.

Manu confirmed what I felt, saying, "The rainbow is a bridge between heaven and earth and visual proof of a Supreme Creator. A rainbow is a reminder that you are a child of God with infinite worth and infinite potential. The rainbow is a symbol of God's promises and God's promise to save you is clear. If you put your faith and trust in Christ, you will be saved in the celestial kingdom. The Bible says, 'For God so loved the world, he gave his only begotten Son, that whosoever believeth in him should not perish, but have everlasting life. For God sent not his Son into the world to condemn the world; but that the world through him might be saved.'[117]

"When I see a rainbow," Manu continued, "I'm reminded of these words of the Savior, 'Be of good cheer, for I will lead you along. The kingdom is yours and the blessings thereof are yours, and the riches of eternity are yours.'[118]

"The Lord doesn't say the celestial kingdom will be yours or could be yours. He says, 'The kingdom is yours and the riches of eternity are yours.' The Savior speaks in the present tense. You can rejoice in your salvation and receive your drink of living water now. The Bibles declares, 'This is the hour to receive God's favor; today is the day to be saved!'"[119]

Manu walked a short distance from the beach into the coconut trees and picked up a palm branch. "The palm branch is a symbol of triumph, waved in ancient Israel to celebrate victories. They were also used to cover paths to welcome royalty. Ancient Israel, as well as Jews today, observe Sukkot, or the Feast of Tabernacles, each year. It's a time to remember the great Jehovah's deliverance of Israel from the bondage of Egypt and the leading of Israel into the promised land. Sukkot is a time to remember and celebrate the Lord providing for Israel as they traveled in the wilderness. During Sukkot, temporary structures with a roof of palm branches called sukkah are built. The sukkah is a symbol of your total dependence on God for your care and sustenance.

"During the festival of Sukkot, palm branches are waved to celebrate all the Lord has done and to acknowledge total dependence on the Lord. As the palm leaves are waved, the 118th Psalm is chanted. The chant includes a shout of hosanna. The Hebrew word 'hosanna,' found at the start of Psalm 118:25, is translated into English as 'save now.'

"The New Testament also records the Hosanna Shout and the waving of palm branches at Jesus's triumphal entry into Jerusalem.[120] This event is now celebrated on Palm Sunday. When the people heard that Jesus was coming to Jerusalem, they took branches of palm trees and went to meet him.[121] The whole multitude of the disciples began to rejoice and praise God with a loud voice for all the mighty works that they had seen.[122] They shouted with joy, 'Hosanna to the Son of David.[123] Hosanna, blessed be the King of Israel that cometh.[124] Hosanna in the highest.'[125]

"The people waved palm branches to recognize Jesus as the great Jehovah who delivered Israel from bondage. The shouts of hosanna also recognized Jesus as the promised Messiah who had come to save them.

"Today, the Hosanna Shout is also done at the dedication of each LDS temple. The white handkerchief has the same symbolism as the palm branch. You wave the handkerchief to remember and celebrate all that the Lord has done. You wave your handkerchief to recognize Jesus Christ as the great Jehovah of the Old Testament and the Messiah of the New Testament—the Savior and Redeemer of the world. The waving of the handkerchiefs and the shouts of 'Hosanna, Hosanna, Hosanna, To God and The Lamb' are a chant of greeting, worship, gratitude, and praise as Jesus Christ makes a triumphant entry into His Holy House.

"Jesus participated in the Feast of Tabernacle during His earthly ministry.[126] Jesus witnessed the waving of palm branches and the shouts of Hosanna as part of the celebration. Jesus also witnessed the practice of the priest pouring water from a gold vase onto the altar of the temple. This was done each day of the Feast of Tabernacle with water taken from the stream of Siloam—water that flowed under the temple-mountain. Following the pouring of the water on the altar, the words of Isaiah 12:3 were sung, 'With joy you will draw water from the springs of salvation.'[127]

"Following this part of the Feast of Tabernacle, Jesus declared Himself the spring of salvation saying, 'If any man thirst, let him come unto me, and drink. He that believeth on me, as the scripture hath said, out of his belly shall flow rivers of living water.'[128] In the Old Testament, the Lord Jehovah declared, 'I will pour water upon him that is thirsty.'[129] Now, the Lord Jehovah in the flesh, as Jesus the Christ, offered living water to those who would believe on Him. Jesus's offer of living water was a plain and open claim of Messiahship. Jesus clearly identified Himself as the great Jehovah and the spring of living water and salvation. After such a pronouncement, His hearers were faced with two choices: either He was a blasphemer and liar, or He was in fact the God of Israel.[130]

"You're each faced with this same choice." Manu declared, looking each of us in the eyes. "Do you believe that Jesus is the great Jehovah of the Old Testament?"

Some of the young men fidgeted uncomfortably. They realized Manu was talking to them.

"Do you believe that Jesus is the Messiah? Do you believe that Jesus is your Savior and your Redeemer? Do you believe that Jesus is the spring of living water and salvation? If you want to answer yes to these questions, please pick up a palm branch."

Though a few hesitated, each of the young men and I picked up a palm branch. Manu smiled as he, too, picked up a branch near his feet.

Manu continued, "You should each wave a palm branch and shout Hosanna to invite Christ to make a triumphant entry into your life. Begin to wave your palm branch to declare that Jesus Christ is your

Savior, your Redeemer, and your Messiah. Wave your palm branch to show your gratitude for all that Jesus has done for you. Wave your palm branch to show your faith and trust in the Lord. Wave your palm branch to declare your total dependence upon God."

Manu, the young men, and I each waved our palm branches as Manu spoke. Our movements welcomed in the Holy Spirit. I felt the Spirit of God like a fire was burning.

Without saying a word, Manu gently took each of us by the arm to guide us into a line, shoulder-to-shoulder. Manu took his place at the start of the line and said, "Follow my lead. The shouting of hosanna is a plea for Jesus to save you."

Manu knelt on the ground, placing His palm branch on the ground in front of him and shouted, "Hosanna! Blessed be the name of the Most High God!"[131]

I was next in line. I followed Manu's example and knelt, placing my palm branch before me and next to Manu's as I shouted, "Hosanna! Blessed be the name of the Most High God!"

Each of the young men followed with the Hosanna Shout and placed their palm branch on the ground to form a path of palm leaves.

We knelt in silence. I assumed that they, like me, felt the warmth and overwhelming love of the Lord Jesus Christ.

After a few minutes of silence, Manu rose to his feet and asked in a whisper, "How do you feel?"

One of the young men quietly said, "It's hard to describe, but I felt a warmth fill my body from my head to my toes. I know that Jesus lives and loves me."

The rest of us nodded in agreement, knowing there were not

words to fully describe our feelings.

Manu nodded his head and said, "You have felt the Holy Spirit witnessing that Jesus is the Savior and Redeemer of the world. Jesus has come to quench your thirst for living water. Jesus has come to enter your life, which is your body.[132] When you welcome Christ into your life and put your faith and trust in Him, He becomes a spring of living water inside you, springing up unto everlasting life."[133]

One of the young men ran to Manu and gave him hug. As they embraced, the young man said, "*Mahalo*, Manu. I'll never see this grove, myself, or God the same."

As they released their embrace, the young man shouted with excitement, "Jesus lives!"

Manu smiled and replied, "'Blessed are those who hunger and thirst for righteousness, for they will be filled.'[134] I love you, brother."

The young man replied, "I love you, too."

Manu hugged each of the young men. As they embraced, Manu said to each of them, "I love you, brother."

Each of the young men replied, "I love you, too."

Manu gave me a hug and said, "I love you, brother."

I replied, "I love you, too, brother."

Manu said with emotion, "It's time to leave the grove, but the grove will never leave you. It's a part of you. It's a part of me. It's alive. Many come to this grove and only see coconut trees and a nice place to swim, but those who come with the proper respect experience so much more. The Kapuaiwa Royal Coconut Grove isn't a place to visit. It's home."

CHAPTER 16
KAMAKOU MOUNTAIN

"Peace comes when we go directly to our best friend—the Prince of Peace." [135]

- President Russell M. Nelson

We left the coconut grove, and the young men returned to their truck by the side of the road. Back at the church, we found Naniwaiwai sitting with a small group of people, laughing and talking story. When the group saw that Manu and I had returned, they ended their discussion, gave each other hugs, and departed for home.

"Naniwaiwai, are you up for a trip to the rainforest?" Manu asked.

Naniwaiwai gave me a sidelong glance. "Sure, but do you think Elder Taylor is ready?"

Manu replied, "The rainforest is like a parable. Each person will receive and understand what they are ready for."

Naniwaiwai nodded in agreement.

As we approached the car, Manu said, "Elder Taylor, will you please drive. There are a few things Naniwaiwai and I would like to share with you before we enter the rainforest. It will be helpful if I can refer to my book of notes and the scriptures."

I nodded in agreement and took the driver's seat. After everyone was settled into the car, I began to drive.

Manu said, "The forest of Kamakou is a very secluded and sacred place. Kamakou is Moloka'i's tallest mountain. It's God's home. The people of Moloka'i have worked hard to limit who visits the rainforest to protect and preserve this sacred place. It's a place that's so hidden and pristine that you may feel we're the first people to visit. The three-thousand-acre preserve is the home of more than two hundred rare Hawaiian plants that can be found nowhere else in the world. You will also hear the unique song of the *olomao* and *kawawahie*, two birds nearing extinction."

Naniwaiwai interjected, "We owe a great deal of gratitude and thanks to our *kūpuna* who have protected and preserved this sacred place. Many sacred places of Hawai'i have been destroyed or misused. In fact, several sacred places in Hawai'i are now used for zip lining." Naniwaiwai shook her head. "We have a *kuleana* (God-given responsibility) to protect and preserve this sacred place. I hope there is never a zip line installed on the island of Moloka'i."

"Elder Taylor," Manu asked, "Why do you think some people are more drawn to a zip line in the forest rather than sitting in silence in the forest?"

I shrugged my shoulders and Manu continued. "I think the answer to this question can be found in 2 Nephi 2:14, 'There is a God, and He hath created all things, both the heavens and the earth, and all things that in them are, both things to act and things to be acted upon.' Are you a person who wants to act or a person who wants to be acted upon?"

"I try to be a person who acts," I replied.

"I think many in today's culture have been conditioned to be acted upon," Manu continued. "We're entertained by and acted upon by television and movies. The zip line is another form of entertainment where we're acted upon. With a zip line, little effort and work are involved. You become an object that's acted upon by gravity. Many of the zip lines in Hawaiʻi are called the 'so-and-so zip line experience.' They do create an experience, but it's a fabricated, man-made experience.

"When we place a zip line in the forest, we exchange a natural, God-given experience for an unnatural, man-made one. Sitting in stillness in a rainforest is much more profound, uplifting, and impactful than any zip line, but it requires patience, work, focus, and eyes to see. Many who are a part of mainland culture are afraid of silence. They constantly desire the noise of music, television, movies, and entertainment. They have become conditioned to want to be acted upon.

"If you're considering going on a zip line in Hawaiʻi, I would suggest you ask these questions: 'Do I want a God-given experience or do I want a man-made experience? Do I want to act or do I want to be acted upon? Do I want a zip line experience or do I want to experience ʻāina?

"The way to experience a place is to enter with reverence and respect and to sit in silence with ears to hear. The ʻāina is always speaking to us. Those who zip line through a place miss this experience.

Many come to Hawai'i and never experience the joy and exhilaration that comes when you are silent in the beauty of God's creations.

"I've often heard people say there is nothing to do on Moloka'i. They are looking for entertainment instead of enlightenment. One of the greatest amenities in the world and one of the greatest experiences that Moloka'i has to offer is the thrill ride of silence. In much of the world, it's getting harder and harder to find a place where you can experience silence.

"And beware of confusing quiet with silence, Elder Taylor. They may appear similar, but they are very different. I've been in the temple when it has been quiet and yet, it was still very noisy. I can hear the clutter of people's minds, thoughts, what they're focusing on, and the things they've brought with them into the temple. So even though it's quiet, it's not silent. Stillness is much more than just being quiet. Learning to be still is a skill to learn and develop, and like playing the piano, it takes practice and experience."

I couldn't help but think of my children's struggle to be still during times of reverence. But, are adults any different? Their bodies may not move, but are their minds present and still?

"Stillness can be experienced anywhere. In some places, it's easier to experience. Moloka'i is one of these places. Experiencing the stillness and silence of Moloka'i can help you develop the skill of being still in other places.

"The psalm, 'Be still and know that I am God'[136] contains a command with a promise. The command is to be still. The promise is that you will know God. In a world filled with chatter, clutter, and chaos, it's important to learn to be still and know God.

"The New Testament shares a story of Jesus and His disciples in a storm on the Sea of Galilee. The winds created mighty waves that crashed against their boat. As the boat filled with water, the apostles were afraid they were going to die, so they woke Jesus who was sleeping peacefully. Jesus 'arose, and rebuked the wind, and said unto the sea, Peace, be still. And the wind ceased, and there was a great calm.'[137]

"When you go to the Savior with your storms of life, He says to you as He said to the wind and the sea, 'Peace, be still.' The Lord leads us to stillness and stillness leads to calm and peace."

Manu paused for a moment and then cited the 23rd Psalm, "'The Lord is my shepherd; I shall not want. He maketh me to lie down in green pastures: he leadeth me beside the still waters. He restoreth my soul.'[138]

"We need to spend time alone with Jesus for Him to lead us to stillness. Jesus provides the example for us to follow. The gospels record a pattern of Jesus regularly going to the mountains to pray. In the book of John, we read, '[Jesus] departed again into a mountain himself alone.' In Matthew 14:24 it says, 'When [Jesus] had sent the multitudes away, he went up into a mountain apart to pray: and when the evening was come, he was there alone.'[139]

"The gospels also record a pattern of Jesus taking His disciples to the mountain for silence and communion with God and angels. The gospel of Mark records one of these occasions when Jesus said to His disciples, 'Come away with me by yourselves to a quiet place.'[140]

"In the Book of Mormon, Nephi also shows the example of spending time alone with the Lord. He wrote, 'I, Nephi, did go into the mount oft, and I did pray oft unto the Lord; wherefore the Lord showed unto me great things.'"[141]

Naniwaiwai commented, "Our *kūpuna* regularly observe days of silence and take time alone in the mountains. It's well-known that Gandhi and many Native Americans also regularly observed days of silence. I remember on one of my visits with my grandmother, she said to me, 'I would suggest you talk to God less in prayer and listen more in silence.'

"It's important to regularly spend time with God," Naniwaiwai continued. "During this time, we learn to hear His voice and feel His power and great love. God invites you to come into His presence. We come into His presence through silence. Spending time together is how we build friendships. As you spend time with God, your friendship with Him will grow. 'Quiet time with God is very similar to a special date.'[142]

"You have seen that we breathe deeply before we *pule* (pray), before we enter the temple, and before we enter nature. Breathing is used to still your mind, body, and spirit. Your breath is a gift from God. God brought you to life with His breath—the breath of life. Each breath is a reminder of your total dependence on God and your intimate relationship with Him. He is your Father and you share His breath. King David declared, 'I live and breathe God.'[143] Focused, deep breathing is a *honi* greeting to share breath with God.

"Elder Taylor, it saddens me to see the important practice of being still vanishing from the lives of my grandchildren. They are missing something wonderful and rare in too much of the world today—silence. The culture for many in the mainland is one of always doing something. They are not used to sitting in silence for a day or even an hour. One of Satan's best weapons to keep us from coming to know and love God is to keep us so busy, even doing good things, and so occupied with activities, commitments, and assignments that we don't allow ourselves to be still.[144] In an age of constant noise, distraction, and motion, nothing is as urgent as being still."

Manu began turning the pages of his book of notes and said, "President David O. McKay taught in conference, 'The greatest comfort in this life is the assurance of having a close relationship with God... During these uncertain and crucial times, I should like to emphasize the need for more spirituality, for more meditation and communion with our Father in heaven... I think we pay too little attention to the value of meditation, a principle of devotion... Meditation is the language of the soul... Meditation is one of the most secret, most sacred doors through which we pass into the presence of the Lord.'"[145]

Manu looked up from his notes and Naniwaiwai continued. "To understand Hawaiian culture, you have to learn to be still. Western culture is often so focused on doing that it misses the profound truth that we are not the doer—God is. We are not the Savior—God is. We are not the healer—God is. We are not the teacher—God is. Another promised blessing of stillness is that the Lord will fight your battles. Exodus 14:14 says, 'The Lord will fight for you; you need only to be still.'[146]

"Western culture is often focused on teaching with lecture and information when truth is experienced in silence. God is always teaching, but you have to be still to hear Him. The Book of Mormon describes Christ's voice as 'a still voice of perfect mildness, as if it had been a whisper, and it did pierce even to the very soul.'"[147]

When Naniwaiwai paused, Manu picked up where she left off. "I agree with Naniwaiwai that it's sad to see silence being lost from our culture. We must perpetuate the practice of silence and stillness and more importantly, teach the reasons why these practices are needed. The primary purpose of time in silence and stillness is to build your relationship with your Heavenly Father and the Lord Jesus Christ. Many in Western culture take a consumeristic approach to meditation. They view it as a task they can get something from. To get a better vision of what silence and stillness should be, please picture a mother and daughter arm-in-arm on a leisurely walk. Picture a father and a daughter laughing as they play. Picture a father and a son talking as they skip rocks across a lake. Picture two sisters enjoying nature on a hike. The purpose of stillness and silence is to 'be with' not to 'get from.' It's to cultivate connection and friendship with God."

"Yes, Manu," Naniwaiwai said. "The apostle Paul warned, 'Some…people have missed the most important thing in life—they don't know God.'[148] Jesus Christ should be your best friend.[149] To build this friendship, you need to spend time with Him."

Manu nodded his head in agreement and said, "The Lord himself taught, 'This is life eternal, that they might know thee the only true God, and Jesus Christ, whom thou hast sent.'[150] Every member of the church should receive a testimony that Jesus is the Christ—the Son of God, but this is just the beginning. A testimony of Jesus is the initial step on the path to an ongoing and deepening friendship with the Lord.

Manu turned the pages of his scriptures and said, "In the book of Alma, we read about the missionary service of the sons of Mosiah. As a result of their preaching, 'Thousands were brought to the knowledge of the Lord [and] as many of the Lamanites as believed in their preaching, and were converted unto the Lord, never did fall away.'[151]

"These scriptures describe two major elements of those who never fell away. First, they were brought to a knowledge of the Lord, meaning, they received a testimony of Jesus. Second, they were converted to the Lord, meaning, they developed a relationship and friendship with Jesus. Notice that this verse doesn't say they were brought to a knowledge of the Church. It says they were brought to a knowledge of the Lord. Notice that it doesn't say they were converted to the Church. It says they were converted to the Lord. Those who are converted to the Church may fall away, but those who are converted to the Lord Jesus Christ will never fall away.

"Elder D. Todd Christofferson, an apostle of the Lord Jesus Christ, taught in General Conference, 'We do not strive for conversion to the Church but to Christ and His gospel.'[152] The Book of Mormon expresses it best when it says that the people 'were converted unto the Lord, and were united unto the church of Christ.'"[153]

Manu continued, "Sadly, many Latter-day Saints who are baptized fall away because they are converted to the Church instead of being converted to Christ. The most common phrase heard in testimony meeting is, 'I know the Church is true,' but it should be, 'I know Jesus is the Christ' and 'Jesus is my friend.' The statement,

'I know that Jesus is the Christ' is a statement of testimony. 'Jesus is my friend' is a statement of conversion. When we help those who are baptized become converted to the Lord, like the Lamanites, they will never fall away."

Manu turned from the Book of Mormon to the New Testament and continued. "During His mortal ministry, Jesus taught about His second coming with the parable of the ten virgins. 'And then, at that day before the Son of Man comes, the kingdom of heaven shall be likened unto ten virgins, who took their lamps and went forth to meet the bridegroom. And five of them were wise, and five of them were foolish. They that were foolish took their lamps and took no oil with them; but the wise took oil in their vessels with their lamps. While the bridegroom tarried, they all slumbered and slept. And at midnight there was a cry made: Behold, the bridegroom cometh! Go ye out to meet him! Then all those virgins arose and trimmed their lamps. And the foolish said unto the wise, Give us of your oil; for our lamps are gone out. But the wise answered, saying, Lest there be not enough for us and you, go you rather to them that sell, and buy for yourselves. And while they went to buy, the bridegroom came; and they that were ready went in with him to the marriage, and the door was shut. Afterward came also the other virgins, saying, Lord, Lord, open unto us. But he answered and said, Verily, I say unto you, You know me not.'"[154]

Manu continued, "The ten virgins are symbolic of active members of The Church of Jesus Christ of Latter-day Saints who are looking for Christ's return. The lamp represents the covenant of baptism. Baptism is the beginning of our covenant relationship with

Christ. At baptism, we take upon us the name of Christ. We become one with Christ. We become perfect in Christ. We are married to Christ. Just like a marriage, our relationship with Christ should be nourished and developed. All ten virgins having lamps symbolize that all were baptized members of the church. However, only five of the virgins had oil in their lamps. The oil in the lamps is symbolic of our relationship with Christ. A relationship must be developed and isn't something you can share or receive from another. The five virgins with no oil in their lamps are symbolic of members of the church who haven't developed their relationship with Jesus. Members of the church who haven't developed a relationship with the Savior will hear the sad words, 'You know me not.'"

"This seems hard to imagine," I said. "Are you telling me that half of the active members of the church will not know Jesus when He comes?"

"I don't know that the parable is giving an exact percentage, Elder Taylor," Manu answered, "but it's clearly teaching that there will be two groups of saints—a group that will know the Savior and a group that will not."

Still somewhat puzzled I asked, "How can those who are members of Christ's church not know Christ?"

Manu answered, "Sometimes, the best way to see the future is to study the past. You can better understand the Lord's second coming by better understanding His first coming recorded in the New Testament. If there was any group that should have celebrated the ministry of Jesus of Nazareth, it should have been the Pharisees. The Pharisees studied the scriptures. They followed the commandments.

They went to synagogue every week. They followed the prophets. They served in the temple. They were righteous. They were exactly obedient. They were looking for the Lord to come. The Pharisees were active members of the church. The Pharisees knew about the Lord, but they didn't know the Lord. They had built a relationship with the church, but they hadn't built a relationship with the Lord. They knew about the Savior and His commandments, but they didn't know the Savior.

"Sadly, some members of The Church of Jesus Christ of Latter-day Saints have a testimony of the Lord, but they don't have a relationship with Him. Like the Pharisees, they go to church every week, keep the commandments, follow the prophet, and attend the temple regularly. They may have a relationship with Christ's church, but this doesn't guarantee that they will have a relationship with Christ. Many members and leaders of the New Testament church didn't recognize Jesus at His first coming. Likewise, many members and leaders of His latter-day church won't recognize Jesus at His Second Coming."

Manu closed his scriptures and we drove in silence for a moment. The Spirit struck my heart with the truth of his words. I felt saddened by the reality that many Latter-day Saints don't know the Lord. As I felt the pain of this reality, my heart ached for my brothers and sisters, and tears welled up in my eyes.

Manu then broke the silence with a piercing question. "Elder Taylor, at the Second Coming, will you know the Savior?"

I waited. I knew what I wanted to answer, but I also wanted to take a moment to ponder if I truly would know Him.

As I pondered on Manu's question, Naniwaiwai said, "Elder Taylor, I have some more questions for you. How can you come to know the Savior and how can you strengthen your friendship with Him?"

Several thoughts came into my mind as I considered her questions, but before I could answer, she asked me a third question. "Elder Taylor, how often do you say to your wife, 'I love you'?"

"Every day." I didn't need to think about that one.

Naniwaiwai replied with another question. "When was the last time you told the Savior, 'I love you'?

"Since Jesus is your marriage partner, doesn't it make sense that you should regularly tell Him, 'I love you'? Partaking of the sacrament is a time each Sunday to be still and know God. It's a time to ponder on the grace, mercy, and forgiveness of the Lord. May I suggest that after you eat of Christ's body and drink of His blood, you take a moment to say, 'Jesus, I love you.' I would suggest you say these words out loud. Now, I know you will be in Church so you will say it very softly and with reverence, but it's important to say the words out loud. Try doing this each week and see what it does for your relationship with Jesus."

The sacrament had always held great meaning for me, but I hadn't considered verbally expressing my love to the Savior.

We drove in silence for a few minutes, pondering on the wisdom that had been shared and enjoying the warmth of the Spirit that filled the car. As we approached a sign that read Kamakou Preserve, Manu said, "Elder Taylor, please pull over to the side of the road."

As I pulled to the side of the road, Manu said, "I asked you to pull over so we can ask permission before entering this area. Kamakou is a sacred place. Once we enter the Kamakou Preserve, we'll be silent."

We exited the car and followed the same pattern we had when entering other places on the island. Once we received permission to enter, we returned to the car and continued our drive in silence.

The narrow, bumpy, dirt road rocked us back and forth in our seats. As we ascended the mountain, the landscape began to change dramatically. When we had begun our drive, we were on the dry side of the island, surrounded by the desert landscape of short, dry trees, wheat-colored grasses, rocks, and open space. We were now enveloped by lush trees and plants, with the trees getting progressively greener and denser the higher we climbed. The road was also transforming. What had started as a dry and bumpy roadway was now a slick and muddy path covered with water-filled potholes that sprayed their contents at us as we passed over them.

After an hour of driving through spectacular scenery, we came to a clearing. Manu directed me to pull to the side of the road at the Waikolu Valley lookout. We hadn't seen any other cars or people during our drive to the lookout, so it wasn't a surprise to find ourselves alone. It was a beautiful, clear Sabbath afternoon. I walked to the edge of the cliff and peered to the valley floor 3,600 feet below. The valley was accented by numerous waterfalls. The lush, green walls of the valley continued for miles before ending at the ocean.

A freshness and purity filled the air, and although both the mountains and valley were still, they weren't silent. The melodies of countless birds in neighboring and distant trees permeated the air while the calming sounds of flowing water emanated from the waterfalls. This was Molokaʻi the way God intended.

Manu, Naniwaiwai, and I each found spots where we could sit and meditate. I tried to apply what I had just been taught about being still and spending time with my Heavenly Father and the Lord Jesus Christ. All through the drive, I'd craved the opportunity to sit and think. There was so much to take in that my mind and heart needed a chance to ponder. I wished everyone could experience Hawaiʻi this way.

We sat in stillness and meditation. I prayed quietly, sat still, and waited. After about thirty minutes, I experience the fulfillment of the promise "Be still and know that I am God." I didn't see the Lord, but I received a witness more powerful than sight. I felt His love, peace, kindness, and power. Satan works hard to prevent silence and stillness to keep us from connecting with God. Satan knows that if you're still, you will know there is a God. Having this experience reinforced why Naniwaiwai and Manu were so troubled to see stillness and meditation being forgotten by so many. Stillness unlocks the door to revelation. However, many are not still long enough to open the door. Meditation helps to clear your mind of your own thoughts and distractions, so God can speak to you.

Our silence continued as we drove down the mountain, leaving the dirt roads of the preserve behind us and returning to the highway back to Hālawa Valley. The thought came to my mind that I should write. I quickly followed the Spirit's prompting and pulled out my spiral notebook and pen. As I looked at the blank page, words began to flow into my mind. After writing for a few minutes, the inspiration came to an end, and I closed my notebook.

"Elder Taylor, what did you write?" Naniwaiwai inquired, breaking the prolonged silence.

"I wrote the words of the Savior in a poem called 'Children of Light.'"

"Would you be willing to share the poem with us?" Naniwaiwai asked.

I nodded by head, opened my notebook, and read:

Children of Light

I am the light and the life of the world.

Live in the light of grace. My grace is sufficient for you, and you shall be lifted up at the last day.

Live in the light of tranquility. My yoke is easy and My burden is light.

Live in the light of family. Love one another, as I have loved you.

Live in the light of friendship. You are my friend, and you shall have an inheritance with Me.

Live in the light of generosity. Freely ye have received, freely give.

Live in the light of gratitude. He who receiveth all things with thankfulness shall be made glorious.

Live in the light of creation. I have created the earth to please the eye and to gladden the heart.

Live in the light of abundance. The earth is full. There is enough and to spare.

Live in the light of miracles. I am a God of miracles. I am the same yesterday, today, and forever.

Live in the light of Aloha. Out of Zion, the beautiful place of Aloha, I shine brightly.

Be the children of light.

After a short silence, Manu commented, "I have found that one visual characteristic more than any other embodies the peace and tranquility we all yearn for. That characteristic is light."[155]

Naniwaiwai nodded her head in agreement and said, "The people of Moloka'i are beautiful and bright, for they are the children of light."

CHAPTER 17
KALAUPAPA

"We are happiest when we are thinking about someone other than ourselves."

- President Russell M. Nelson

The evening was spent in contemplation and, for me, some excitement. We arose early in the morning because today, we were to ride mules to Kalaupapa. While I enjoyed my scripture study, meditation time, and a simple breakfast, I was more than ready when we started our drive to the stable. It was just Manu and me since Naniwaiwai chose to stay home and work in her *kalo* fields.

"How long of a drive is it to Kalaupapa?" I asked as we began.

"Oh, about sixty to ninety minutes," Manu answered. "It will give me time to tell you about this unique and sacred place."

I nodded my head, excited to be taught.

"Kalaupapa is an isolated peninsula lying below the towering cliffs of Molokaʻi's mountainous north shore. These sea cliffs are the highest in the world, at over three thousand vertical feet. The Kalaupapa Peninsula is divided into three *ahupuaʻa* (land divisions): Kalaupapa, Makanalua, and Kalawoa. The region was formed well after the rest of the island by lava flows from Kauhakō Crater, which rests prominently in the center of the peninsula. A small lake, which is eight hundred feet deep, is found inside the crater. Two *heiau* and a *hōlua* slide are located on the crater."

"What's a *hōlua* slide?" I asked.

Manu answered, "Hawaiians love sports of all kinds. *Heʻe hōlua* was a prestigious sport played in ancient Hawaiʻi, mostly during *Makahiki*, the Hawaiian New Year Festival. It tested the balance, strength, and courage of riders as they hurled headfirst down a steep decline at speeds of more than sixty miles per hour while riding a sled."

"Sounds like snow sledding," I said, "just minus the snow."

"Precisely, Elder Taylor," Manu said smiling. "A *hōlua* slide was built on the side of a steep hill and ranged in length from a few hundred feet to over a mile. Rocks were covered with dirt, grass, and *kukui* (candlenut) oil to create a slick surface. The riders rode on sleds that consisted of two long and narrow runners held apart by crosspieces, which were lashed together with coconut fiber. These sleds were about a foot in width, up to fourteen feet long, and could weigh as much as fifty pounds."

"Sign me up," I responded enthusiastically. "Sounds like fun."

"It was fun, but it was also very dangerous," Manu commented.

"More dangerous than riding a mule down a cliff?" I asked.

Manu laughed and answered, "Naniwaiwai and I are both friends with the family that owns the mule tour company. They have been doing mule rides for decades and have yet to have a mule jump off the cliff. There is no such thing as a suicidal mule."

I chuckled and asked, "Have you done this mule ride before?"

"Yes, I have, many years ago. It's a scary ride for some, but it's definitely safer than *he'e hōlua*," Manu answered with a smile.

He continued, "Another favorite sport in ancient Hawai'i was surfing. Kalaupapa is said to have been the favorite surfing spot of Moloka'i chiefs. However, sled racing and surfing came to an end in Kalaupapa in 1865, when King Kamehameha V established Kalaupapa as a leper colony to prevent the spread of the feared disease. Because of its extreme isolation, Kalaupapa was chosen as the location to quarantine lepers. The peninsula is surrounded by rough water on three sides and large sea cliffs on its fourth. The Hawaiian people, with little immunity to introduced diseases, were susceptible to leprosy. One in fifty contracted the disease. From 1866 to 1969, over eight thousand people were sent to Kalaupapa to die. At the height of the epidemic, over a thousand patients lived in the colony.[156]

"The Hawaiian Kingdom had seen the foreign diseases of smallpox, measles, chicken pox, polio, influenza, cholera, whooping cough, mumps, and tuberculosis kill thousands of Hawaiians. The fear of disease was very real, and there wasn't a single Hawaiian family that didn't have someone close to them taken by one of these foreign diseases. The fear of another disease spreading and killing thousands led to a drastic law to quarantine those diagnosed with leprosy to Kalaupapa. Even with the quarantine in place, leprosy still took the lives of thousands of Hawaiians.

"It's estimated that at the time of Captain Cook's arrival in Hawai'i in 1778, the total population of the Hawaiian islands was about 700,000. By 1920 only 25,000 native Hawaiians remained.

The colossal number of premature deaths from disease was extremely disruptive to the transfer of the knowledge and practice of Aloha from one generation to the next. During this period, not only were an enormous number of Hawaiian lives lost, but there was also a substantial loss of Hawaiian knowledge, culture, history, language, and wisdom. Thankfully, for the past several decades there has been a resurgence of the Hawaiian population, culture, and language. Elder Taylor, I believe you're one of many the Lord is using to continue this resurgence."

At times, I wondered why the Lord would use a man from Idaho of all places, but He'd used unlikely vessels before. For the rest of the drive, Manu shared with me many of the people, places, and events involved in preserving and restoring pieces of Hawaiian history, language, and culture. As he spoke, I had the feeling that in the years to come, we would visit many of the places and people he spoke of.

Manu suddenly changed the subject saying, "We're getting close. Let me tell you a little about Buzzy Sproat, the owner of the mule tour company. Buzzy is the *paniolo* (cowboy) of the Pacific. I like to call him Mr. Aloha. He is full of life and loves people. He is a master storyteller and loves to talk story. He has been taking visitors from all over the world to Kalaupapa for forty years. Buzzy is in his seventies, although you would never know it. He shows no signs of slowing down and often still does the tours five days a week."

Manu pulled off the road and parked in front of an old sheet metal building. Rust spotted the structure and old items were propped against one side. Tall grass reached high, nearly covering a dirty window, but Manu started to get out of the car.

"Why have we stopped here?" I asked.

"This is the stable where Uncle Buzzy keeps the mules," Manu responded.

It was definitely not what I had envisioned. And this was the man who would guide us down a cliff face on a mule? I followed Manu to the door of the stable and followed him inside.

Buzzy was inside grooming a mule. As he turned to see who had entered, a big smile spread across his face. "Howzit, braddah?" Buzzy boomed. "It has been way too long."

Buzzy quickly walked over to Manu and gave him an enormous hug.

Buzzy was short with muscles built from heavy use. He had a white beard and a smile replete with Aloha. His hands were firm and rough—weathered from years of work. He wore an old, black cowboy hat, brown cowboy boots with spurs, a denim jacket, and a red bandana around his neck. His countenance radiated joy and love. Despite my initial reservations upon our arrival, I felt connected to him instantly.

Turning to me he said, "You must be Elder Taylor."

I nodded. "I'm excited and honored to meet the famous Buzzy Manu has been telling me about."

Buzzy replied, "Well, I'm not sure what he told you, but I can assure you that I'm not famous. But I'll give you an adventure of a lifetime today, an adventure you will never forget, an experience that will change how you see the world."

Manu nodded his head in agreement. "Buzzy, will there be

anyone else joining us today?"

"No, no," Buzzy answered. "When Naniwaiwai told me she had invited you to the island, I offered to take you and Elder Taylor for free as my guests. It's an honor to help Naniwaiwai. Once today was selected for your mule ride, I closed reservations, so it would just be the three of us."

Manu smiled. "*Mahalo,* my friend."

"No worries, braddah. I've been looking forward to spending a day with you and Elder Taylor. Oh, I almost forgot." Buzzy grabbed a lei from behind the counter. He placed the lei over Manu's head while giving him a warm Aloha. He grabbed a second lei and repeated the process for me. "These are gifts made by my wife for our special guests today."

Manu and I both offered Aloha in return, thanking Buzzy for his hospitality and kindness.

As Buzzy returned to grooming one of the mules, he said, "One of my favorite parts of the day is matching the mules to the riders. Each mule has a unique spirit and personality. The proper match is very important."

Buzzy paused his work for a moment and looked at me, scanning me from head to toe. "Elder Taylor, I think Alika will be perfect for you."

Buzzy then gazed back and forth between Manu and the mules and said, "Manu, I think I'll have you ride Li'i today. Li'i is short for *ali'i,* which you of course know, means chief. Li'i will be honored to carry a Hawaiian chief today."

Buzzy turned to me and asked, "Elder Taylor, what do you

know about mules?"

"Very little," I answered.

"Have you ever ridden a mule?" Buzzy asked.

"I've not," I replied.

Buzzy smiled with excitement. "Well, you're in for a real treat. Alika will take good care of you. Are you nervous at all?"

I shook my head no and answered, "I wouldn't say I'm nervous, but I'm curious what it will be like riding a mule down a cliff." However, I did wonder what my wife would think.

"Many of our visitors are worried and nervous. I understand how being on a mule on the edge of a cliff could cause people some worry, but it's very safe. We've made this trip thousands of times and have yet to have a mule jump," Buzzy said with a smile.

"Mules don't scare easily like horses. A mule is a hybrid animal that comes from crossing a jack (male donkey) and a mare (female horse). Many people who come here are horse people who think mules are dumb. By the time they get back at the end of the day, they are mule people and respect the mule. The mule isn't going to win the Kentucky Derby, but it's not going fall off the cliff either. Come help me saddle the mules and we'll get on our way."

Manu and I helped Buzzy saddle the mules. Buzzy stroked and spoke gently to each mule as he saddled it. I could tell that each was a special friend. It was a simple, old stable but it was filled with compassion and love. My initial thought as we pulled up was that this was a worthless, abandoned building, but I was clearly wrong. Too often, we judge people and places by what we see, when we should judge by what we feel. We see the external when we should seek to see the internal. "Man looketh on the outward appearance, but the Lord looketh on the heart."[157]

After we had the mules saddled, we led them out of the stable into an open, fenced, grassy area. There were two platforms with stairs, making it easy for riders to mount. Buzzy directed me to the platform, and I was the first onto my mule. Manu was next, followed by Buzzy.

Buzzy led the way onto the highway that ran along the stable. Since the mules knew where they were going, my only job was to enjoy the ride. As my mule came to the side of Buzzy's mule, I started to ask him a question. "Buzzy—"

Before I could even begin my sentence, Buzzy interrupted me saying, "Please call me Uncle. Everyone who comes to my stable is a part of my family. You're 'ohana."

I nodded my head and started again, "Uncle, have you ever thought about retiring?"

Uncle Buzzy laughed. "Why would I stop doing what I love? Retirement is a creation of the Western world. It's not Hawaiian. I'll continue to do this for as long as I can. I'll be one of those guys who dies with his boots on. It's been a great life, and I wouldn't trade all this for anything."

I marveled at how much he enjoyed working and how much he loved people, his mules, and the places of Moloka'i. After a short distance riding down the paved highway, we turned onto a dirt road. We traveled on the dirt road under a beautiful tree canopy. After traveling about a mile, Uncle Buzzy paused at the sign for the Kalaupapa trail, allowing our mules to come together.

Uncle Buzzy said, "The Guinness Book of World Records documents these sea cliffs as the highest in the world. We'll be riding down 1,700 feet of spectacular landscape. The trail is just over three miles with twenty-six switchbacks. It's better than any ride in Disneyland."

Uncle Buzzy laughed and started his mule down the trail. I couldn't help but smile. Alika and Liʻi followed Uncle Buzzy in a single file line. Uncle Buzzy had made this trip hundreds of times but his excitement wasn't diminished. He was like a boy on Christmas morning, excited for what the day would bring. As we rode, I contemplated Uncle Buzzy's excitement and enthusiasm for this journey, despite traveling down this same trail for over forty years.

As I pondered, I thought, "Is a boy's excitement reduced because he has experienced Christmas in years past? No! In fact, the past Christmases may actually increase his excitement as he recalls the joy he's experienced before. The boy looks with anticipation and excitement for what this Christmas will bring."

The beginning of the trail was wider than I anticipated, perhaps five feet across with rocks and stairs built to prevent erosion and assist hikers. Portions of the trail narrowed to two or three feet. The surroundings were a vibrant green from the regular rainfall, but this also meant a muddy trail, pocked with holes that were filled with brown water. Not only was the terrain wet, but portions of the trail were extremely steep, compelling me to hold on tightly to my mule and to lean back to prevent myself from falling headlong over the front of my mule.

My mule preferred to walk on the very edge of the cliff in an attempt to avoid the muddy trail. This provided breathtaking views of the drop below, but it wasn't a trip for the faint of heart. On one of the switchbacks, Alika's hooves moved to the very edge of the trail. The sharp edge moved us away from the cliff wall. My eyes played tricks on me and made it feel as though we floated in the air. I couldn't see the cliff wall, only the ground 1,500 feet below. My hands clutched the saddle, turning my knuckles white. I wondered if I was to be the first to ride a mule over the edge. My heart pounded so hard I was sure Uncle Buzzy or Manu would ask about the sound. Was I going to die? Although my heart was filled with fear and dread, Alika, seemingly unfazed, continued plodding around the switchback. I could see solid ground beneath Alika's feet. I released a huge sigh of relief, and my moment of terror passed.

The beauty of the scenery, ocean, and Kalaupapa Peninsula were remarkable. I spotted a mountain goat on the cliffs above me and a group of wild boars in a wooded area of trees further down the trail. Uncle Buzzy whistled elaborate melodies that acted as the background melody to our adventure. At the bottom of the trail, we reached a pristine beach that led to a large, flat, open field of green grass, with the ocean bordering our left and the cliffs on our right.

We guided our mules into a fenced area where they could rest while we explored the rest of Kalaupapa. We helped Uncle Buzzy get the mules comfortable and headed for our next method of transportation: an old, orange school bus that was parked in the field.

"Uncle, have you driven this bus before?" Manu asked.

Uncle Buzzy smiled. "I've led countless tours over the years. I fill in wherever I'm needed. Although I think the tour I'm going to give you today will be different from any tour I've seen and any tour I've given."

"Why do you say that?" Manu asked.

"On our journey down the cliffs today, the Spirit told me to give you and Elder Taylor a tour called, 'A Model of Ministry.' I confess that I'm not entirely sure what I'm supposed to share and how I'm supposed to share it."

Manu replied, "This scripture is being brought to my mind, 'Open your mouths and they shall be filled, and you shall become even as Nephi of old, who journeyed from Jerusalem in the wilderness.'"[158]

Uncle Buzzy nodded his head. "That scripture uses the pronoun 'they' so you and Elder Taylor will be helping me, right?"

Manu smiled. "I think the Lord will guide each of us and fill our minds and our mouths. By the Holy Spirit, we'll be taught what the Lord wants us to learn."

There was a profound peace and solemnity that radiated from the 'āina. I could feel this was a holy place like nowhere else in the world. I was filled with excitement about being taught by God in this unique area of the world.

We loaded onto the bus, with Uncle Buzzy taking the driver's seat while Manu and I took the front seats.

I looked eagerly out the window as we drove into the small town of Kalaupapa.

Uncle Buzzy slowed the bus to a stop and while pointing out the window said, "This is the Kalaupapa wharf."

We climbed out of the bus and walked out onto a small, concrete dock. A refreshing, salty breeze filled the air. I walked to the end of the pier. I watched as the tranquil, blue ocean turned to white crested waves that crashed into the black lava rock of the shore. Majestic palm trees led to the sea cliffs we'd just descended. As I examined the massive cliffs from the pier, the terrain seemed impossible to travel by mule, and yet we had. The view of the lush, green sea cliffs nestled between sky and waves was wondrous. It was a scene that even the most skilled photographer couldn't fully capture with a camera. The true beauty of Kalaupapa was felt more than seen. Although there was beauty in every direction, the real beauty needed more than physical eyes to be seen.

Uncle Buzzy joined Manu and me at the end of the pier and said, "Kalaupapa is so isolated that even today, freight is only delivered once a year by barge. There's only one barge in the state small enough to fit into Kalaupapa's narrow harbor, and in addition to this, there is only a short window of time in the summer when the rough water is calm enough for the barge to safely dock. It can take the barge over an hour to slowly maneuver around the reef and rocks into this small wharf.

"Residents look forward to barge day when their personal orders are delivered. It's their Christmas in July. The barge also delivers a year's worth of equipment, gasoline, and nonperishable food supplies. For 364 days of the year, this pier is quiet with no activity like today. But on barge day, the wharf becomes a flurry of activity. Barge day is a big occasion with most residents coming to the wharf to greet the barge and see what was ordered.[159]

We made our way back onto the bus and Uncle Buzzy began to drive. "I think we will head over to Kalawao. There are two main settlements on the peninsula: Kalaupapa, where we are now, is on the west side and Kalawao is on the east side. Most of the residents now live in the Kalaupapa settlement, so the peninsula is typically referred to as the Kalaupapa Peninsula, even though its correct name is the Makanalua Peninsula. This peninsula is only about two miles wide and three miles long. Kalaupapa is one of the subdivisions of the peninsula.

As Uncle Buzzy spoke, I realized that although we hadn't been in Kalaupapa very long, I had yet to see any other people.

"Uncle Buzzy," I said, "does anyone still live in Kalaupapa?"

"Oh, yes," Uncle Buzzy replied. "There are eighty residents currently living here. This number includes a handful of former leprosy patients, federal employees who work on preservation projects, and some state-employed health workers. All former patients were granted permission to leave the colony in 1969 but a few of them have chosen to stay."

As we drove, I gazed out the window, looking at the occasional buildings and houses scattered along the road. Once we left the small town of Kalaupapa, there was open green space on both sides of the road. Cars were as scarce as people, so we had the smooth, paved road to ourselves. Even though this was a place with a history of much suffering and death, the ʻāina radiated peace and love. I couldn't help but wonder how that could be.

CHAPTER 18
THE PŪ HALA TREE

"Foxes have holes and birds of the air have nests, but the Son of Man has nowhere to lay His head." [160]

- Jesus Christ

Uncle Buzzy eventually pulled the bus to the side of the road. As I glanced around, I wondered why we were stopping since I didn't see anything in the area. Uncle Buzzy led Manu and me under the shade of a beautiful tree. He pulled some notes from his pocket and asked, "Elder Taylor, what do you know about Father Damien?"

"I've read a little about him," I replied.

"Well, I'll do my best to share with you the life of this devoted servant of the Lord. Let's start at the beginning." Uncle Buzzy pulled out a small notebook. "Joseph De Veuster, who would eventually become known as Father Damien, was born in 1840 in Belgium as the seventh child in his family.[161] Joseph wanted to follow in the footsteps of his sisters, Eugénie and Pauline, who became nuns and his brother, Auguste, who became a priest. In 1858, Joseph wrote in a letter to his parents, 'I must write you on this Christmas Day on which I have been given certain knowledge that God wants me to leave the world and enter the religious life. You must not think, my dear father and mother, that this is just my own choice; I have been impelled to it by Divine Providence. I cannot imagine that you will hinder me. If God calls me, I must obey. God has destined me for this call since I was a child.'[162]

"Joseph stayed with his brother and eagerly learned from him. As they discussed Joseph's future, Auguste recommended that his brother join him in serving in The Congregation of the Sacred Hearts. Joseph accepted the invitation and was assigned to the choir brothers, whose responsibilities included perpetual adoration of the Blessed Sacrament, teaching in the colleges of the congregations, and care of the chapel.[163] To signify his new life as a servant of the Lord Jesus Christ, Joseph received the new name Brother Damien.

"The Catholic mission in Hawai'i requested that more people be sent, and Damien volunteered to go in the place of his brother, who had been selected to go, but became ill and was unable to make the journey. Damien's request was granted and he was sent to Hawai'i with sixteen others: one priest, three future priests (of whom Damien was one), three lay brothers, and ten nuns.[164]

"Damien was at sea for one hundred and forty days before stepping ashore at Honolulu Harbor on March 19, 1864. The Bishop, Monseigneur Maigret, was eager to have Damien and his two companions become priests, so he sent them to the Catholic MTC—a college just outside of the town. During the next two months, Damien completed his theological studies and studied the Hawaiian language. The language came easily to him and he quickly became fluent in Hawaiian. On May 21, at the Cathedral of Our Lady of Peace,

Damien was ordained into the priesthood at the age of twenty-four. From this time forward, he was known as Father Damien. His first calling was on the Big Island, where he spent eight years.

"Father Damien wrote to his parents following his ordination saying, 'Now I am a priest, now I am a missionary. I wonder how I can fulfill my duties as a missionary priest. Never forget this poor priest searching night and day for the lost sheep. Pray continually for me. I am surrounded by so many spiritual hazards, but if the Lord is with me, I have nothing to fear, and in the words of St. Paul, I can do all in Christ who strengtheneth me. Goodbye, my beloved parents. Though our bodies are apart, let prayer keep us one in spirit. Have no uneasiness about me, for when one serves God, one is happy anywhere.'[165]

"During this time, the Kingdom of Hawai'i was facing a public health crisis. Thousands of Hawaiians had died of influenza, syphilis, and other ailments brought to the islands by foreign traders and sailors. One of the diseases plaguing the islands was leprosy, also known as Hansen's disease. Leprosy is one of the oldest diseases in recorded history and is caused by a chronic, progressive bacterial infection. The bacteria responsible for leprosy multiply very slowly, so a person may be infected for years before the first appearance of symptoms—skin sores, nerve damage, and muscle weakness—begin to appear. As the bacteria grows, nerve damage progresses until there is loss of feeling in the extremities. The skin sores advance to severe disfigurement and eventually parts of the body, such as the ears, fingers, toes, and nose, begin falling off.

"At the time, there were no treatments for leprosy. Understandably, fear of the disease was widespread, and by 1865 the Hawaiian Legislature passed the 'Act to Prevent the Spread of Leprosy,' which was then approved by King Kamehameha V. This law required lepers to be quarantined to the settlements of Kalaupapa and Kalawao. Within a year, in 1866, the first leprosy patient was quarantined to Kalaupapa.

"A Hawaiian boy banished to Moloka'i wrote, 'One of the worst things about this illness is what was done to me as a young boy. First, I was sent away from my family. That was hard. I was so sad to go to Kalaupapa. They told me right out that I would die here; that I would never see my family again. I heard them say this phrase, something I will never forget. They said, "This is your last place. This is where you are going to stay and die." That's what they told me. I was a thirteen-year-old kid.'[166]

"Another Hawaiian boy wrote, 'Like the other patients, they caught me at school. It was on the Big Island. I was twelve then. I cried like the dickens for my mother and for my family. But the Board of Health didn't waste no time in those days. They sent me to Honolulu, to Kalihi Receiving Station, real fast. Then they sent me to Kalaupapa. That's where they sent most of us. Most came to die.'[167]

"By the end of 1866, a hundred and forty-one lepers were shipped to Moloka'i. They landed at a beach in Kalaupapa and had to walk three miles to where we now stand in Kalawao. Here, they found a barn-like building without beds, nurses, or doctors. Those with severe cases of leprosy used all their strength to walk to Kalawao and laid on a mat on the bare earth. They remained lying there with their sores unbandaged and their bodies unwashed until they died.

The lepers who were not as badly affected found shelter in the huts of the locals who had lived in Kalawao before being forced by the government to move to make room for the leper colony.[168]

"Hundreds of lepers were sent to Kalaupapa each year. They were given insufficient rations of food, no medical care, and the few homes of prior residents were quickly overcrowded. New arrivals were forced to live in caves and under trees."

"The conditions sound horrible," I said. "I couldn't imagine sending a member of my family, or anyone, into such conditions."

"You're correct, Elder Taylor," Uncle Buzzy replied. "The conditions were horrific. Thankfully, at the start of 1873, the Honolulu newspaper began taking an interest in Moloka'i and began reporting on some of the appalling circumstances and occurrences in Kalaupapa. The newspaper learned that three-hundred-and-eleven of the seven-hundred-and-ninety-seven people forcibly exiled to Kalaupapa had already died in the deplorable conditions.

"Little food was provided to those quarantined to Kalaupapa because they were expected to raise their own food. As reports circulated of the starving lepers, the Board of Health increased the amount and regularity of the food shipment to Kalaupapa. While the increase in food was helpful, much, much more was needed.

"One of the stories reported was of a leper who, on his second day in Kalawao, saw a man come out of his hut pushing a wheelbarrow loaded with what seemed to be a bundle of rags. Out of curiosity, he followed the man to the edge of a small ravine. As he watched the wheelbarrow's contents dumped into the ravine, he heard feeble cries coming from the bundle of rags. The newcomer scrambled into the ravine and found that the rags were covering the decaying body of a man at the point of death. When he protested against the inhumanity, the man was astonished at his making such a fuss about so common an incident."[169]

At first, I sat in stunned silence as Uncle Buzzy finished telling this horrific account, but then I blurted out, "That's unbelievable! Why would they treat each other that way?"

"Elder Taylor," Uncle Buzzy gently replied, "the hard reality was that the sick and the dying abandoned on Kalaupapa didn't have the strength or resources to care for the dying or the dead."

The more I thought about it, the more I realized, they didn't have much choice.

He continued, "About ninety of the lepers in Kalawao were Catholics, so a priest occasionally visited Kalaupapa. The lepers asked the priest to tell the Bishop that it wasn't enough for them to see a priest once a year. The Bishop wanted to send the lepers a full-time priest. However, he didn't feel good about assigning a priest to the leper colony, since he knew such an assignment would be a death sentence.

"On May 4, 1873, a new church was to be consecrated on the island of Maui by the Bishop. Several priests from other islands, including Father Damien, were invited to Maui to meet their Bishop. The Bishop had decided that during one of his meetings with the priests he would ask for a volunteer to serve as the full-time priest of the Moloka'i leper colony. The moment Father Damien heard the Bishop's request, and before any of the other priests could speak, he burst out with, 'I want to go!' The Bishop smiled, gave him an affectionate hug, and agreed that he should go.[170]

"In a letter to his parents, Father Damien shared the account of Isaiah who wrote, 'I heard the voice of the Lord saying Whom shall I send? Then said I, Here am I. Send me.'[171] Damien wrote that he was eager to answer as did the prophet Isaiah, 'Here I am, Lord. Send me.'

"On May 10, 1873, a steamer left the island of Maui. It carried the Bishop, Father Damien, fifty lepers, and some cattle to the secluded settlements on Molokaʻi. All the lepers who could walk were there to welcome the steamer, with the Catholics among them wearing rosary beads around their necks. The Bishop addressed those gathered saying, 'Hitherto, you have been alone and abandoned, but that is all over and done with. Here is someone who will be a father to you. He loves you so intensely that, for your present happiness and for the salvation of your immortal souls, he does not hesitate to become one of you and wishes to live and die with you. This good Father remains at the disposal of his superiors, but be quite sure that we shall never abandon you, neither while you live nor when you die.'[172]

"At the age of thirty-three, Father Damien began his ministry to eight-hundred-and-sixteen lepers. When he arrived on Molokaʻi, he had no home, but he soon learned that having no home was the daily reality of many in the settlement. He refused to sleep indoors until every patient had decent shelter. Night after night, Father Damien curled up to sleep under a tree beside the tiny St. Philomena Church."

Uncle Buzzy looked up into the branches of the tree under which we sat. The tree had distinct characteristics, with aerial roots that spread out like a teepee at the lower portion of the tree. Many branches went up from the root, with a cluster of small palm-like leaves at the top of each branch that formed a canopy over our heads. In the center of each palm-tree-like cluster was a fruit that looked like a small pineapple. "Father Damien slept under a *pū hala* tree like this one every night for months."

Uncle Buzzy continued, "As I mentioned when we first arrived, I was told by the Spirit to give 'The Model of Ministry Tour.' So, what can we learn about ministering from what I've shared?"

After pondering for a moment, I answered, "These words of the Savior come to my mind, 'Foxes have holes and birds of the air have nests, but the Son of Man has nowhere to lay His head.'[173] Father Damien, like Jesus, was more concerned about the needs of others than his own needs."

"Exactly, Elder Taylor," Manu said. "Christ taught that 'The Son of man came not to be ministered unto, but to minister.'[174] The Bible recounts the Lord confronting the apostles about an argument they had." Manu paused to open his scriptures and then read, "'[Jesus] asked them, What was it that ye disputed among yourselves by the way? But they held their peace: for by the way they had disputed among themselves, who should be the greatest. And he sat down, and called the twelve, and saith unto them, If any man desire to be first, the same shall be last of all, and servant of all.'[175]

"In the Jewish society of the day—as in most societies in every generation—there was a huge emphasis on power, position, prestige, and titles. 'Who's number one?' is still the operative question. Because He knew their hearts, Jesus knew about their sinful ambition even before he asked what they were arguing about. And like little children caught misbehaving, they were ashamed to answer him. He chose this moment for an unforgettable teaching experience.[176] The Master taught, 'He that is greatest among you shall be your servant.'"[177]

Uncle Buzzy nodded his head in agreement and said, "Yes. A Christlike minister has the heart of a servant."

Manu commented, "Father Damien dedicated his life to Christ. Exactly what form his life would take he didn't know, but he was willing to serve in whatever way the Lord desired. He was a humble servant of the Lord. Father Damien's willingness to accept the call to Molokaʻi reminds me of the Savior's words in the Garden of Gethsemane, 'Not my will, but thine, be done.'"[178]

Uncle Buzzy spoke reverently and softly, "Christlike ministers put their faith and trust in the Lord. They seek to know and do His will." Uncle Buzzy turned through his pages of notes until he found what he was looking for and continued, "In a letter to his family at the end of his first year on Molokaʻi, Father Damien wrote, 'I find great happiness in serving the Lord in his poor and sick children—who are rejected by others. I love them very much and would willingly give my life for them.'[179] After he contracted leprosy, he wrote in a letter to his Bishop, 'Although there is no doubt that I am a leper, I am resigned, peaceful, and happy in the midst of my people. God knows what is best for me, and every day I gladly say, 'May Thy will be done.'"[180]

Manu commented, "Christlike ministers find joy in serving the Lord and doing His will."

Uncle Buzzy turned through his notes and continued. "The Lord knew He needed a person with certain skills and talents to serve his children in Kalaupapa, so He prepared Father Damien from his youth for his ministry on Molokaʻi. At age thirteen, Father Damien was taken out of school to work on the family farm for five years. His sturdy, powerful body seemed tireless, and the demanding work didn't exhaust him. He felt a desire to not pamper his body, preferring to sleep on a hard board rather than on his softer bed of straw.[181] As a young man, Father Damien was drawn to carpenters, so he spent his free time building and learning the skills of carpentry.

"Father Damien was blessed with a strong body and the ability to work hard for long hours. He made many petitions for wood to build the many needed homes. As the wood arrived, he began building homes and moving those who slept outside, exposed to the wind and rain, into the newly built structures. It wasn't until after everyone in the settlement had a home that he finally built himself a small, sixteen-foot by ten-foot house. In a letter to his mother, Father Damien wrote, 'I'm not ashamed to be a manual laborer for the glory of God. The work habits I developed at home are of immense use to me here.'"[182]

As he spoke, I thought of how the Lord had prepared him to serve. I think the Lord prepares each of us to minister and build the Kingdom of God in different ways.

"Father Damien also built a shelter for twelve orphans. The facility was so attractive to the other boys in the settlement that he soon thereafter decided to build a second, bigger dormitory. In addition to these dormitories, Father Damien also built two schools, one for girls and one for boys.[183]

"Father Damien saw the challenges the residents had obtaining water. Drinking water had to be carried from a stream a long way from their homes. Some of them were too ill to make the journey and had to rely on what their neighbors could spare. Father Damien was often seen carrying buckets of water back to the settlement.

"After exploring the surroundings of the settlement, Father Damien found a deep pool of clear, fresh water at the end of a valley opening. He sent a request that pipes be sent to the island so that he could run water from the spring to Kalawao. When the pipes finally arrived, Father Damien and those suffering from leprosy carried them inland. No engineers came with the pipes, but this wasn't a problem. Father Damien used his craftsman skills to build a water system, with a tap near every home in Kalawao.[184]

"Father Damien also put his skills as a farmer to work. He organized every member of the colony capable of working to assist with planting, caring for, and harvesting crops. They were soon producing far more food than the settlements needed. Father Damien persuaded the Board of Health to buy their surplus produce and the money from these sales went into the pockets of the growers. He even opened a small shop where the colony members could spend the money they had earned. His prices were ridiculously low so that the colony members could afford to purchase items. For those with little or no money, Father Damien gave them what they needed and wanted.

"Father Damien was transforming the colony in profound ways, both on a personal as well as a community level. Being able to provide their own food and earn their own money boosted the morale and confidence of the colonists. They weren't just sick and helpless people who were slowly dying from a horrible disease. They were important contributors to a thriving community. These changes within the people led to spectacular improvements throughout the colony. Just a few years after Father Damien's arrival, Kalawao and Kalaupapa were both very attractive villages.[185] Father Damien reported in 1886, 'I estimate the number of houses at present, both large and small, somewhat over three hundred, nearly all whitewashed and, so far, clean and neat.' During this time period, Father Damien wrote in his journal, 'I have our Lord near to me. I am always happy, and I work with all my heart to make my beloved lepers happy too.'"[186]

Uncle Buzzy paused for a moment before asking, "So, what can we learn about ministering from these stories?"

We sat in silence as we pondered Uncle Buzzy's question, absorbing the feelings of peace, love, and light we had felt as Uncle Buzzy taught us about Father Damien. Manu was the first to speak. "A few years ago, I took a trip to the Salt Lake Temple. While I was there, I had the impression to place my hand on the granite walls to learn from these sacred stones. As I placed my hand on the stone, I was taught. I felt that the stone used in the Salt Lake Temple was formed during the creation of the world for this very purpose. The granite boulders that would become the walls of the Salt Lake Temple were foreordained and prepared for this very purpose.

"Just as the Lord prepared the granite for the Salt Lake Temple, He prepared Father Damien for his Moloka'i ministry. Becoming a minister of the Lord Jesus Christ requires preparation. Jesus spent thirty years preparing for His full-time ministry. The New Testament tells us that Jesus 'grew, and waxed strong in spirit, filled with wisdom: and the grace of God was upon him. Jesus increased in wisdom and stature, and in favor with God and man.'[187]

"Father Damien prepared for His ministry with years of hard work and learning to farm, build, and love. Sleeping on a hard board in his youth prepared him for his nights sleeping on the hard ground of Molokaʻi. It's not a coincidence that this mighty model of ministry was a carpenter, like the Master he served. When a volunteer was asked to go to Molokaʻi, Father Damien exclaimed quickly, 'I want to go,' feeling this was the ministry the Lord had prepared him for."

As Manu spoke, my own mind was filled. "I'm reminded of one of my favorite quotes from President Nelson," I began. "'There is no shortcut to excellence and competence. Education is the difference between wishing you could help other people and being able to help them.'[188] Father Damien's skills and experience as a farmer and carpenter enabled him to help those suffering from leprosy by building homes, creating water systems, and cultivating farms."

Uncle Buzzy nodded his head with a smile. "Christlike ministers develop the gifts and talents the Lord has given them. Any other thoughts?"

I answered, "I'm reminded of a talk given by Elder Bednar on the spiritual gift of being quick to observe.[189] Father Damien had the gift of observation. He was quick to see a person in need and as an instrument in the hands of the Lord, he worked to satisfy the identified need."

Uncle Buzzy again nodded his approval and said, "Yes. Ministry is about fulfilling needs. A Christlike minister has the gift of observation and works to fulfill the needs of others."

CHAPTER 19
THE COVE AT KALAWAO

"The Church partners with agencies such as the Red Cross, Catholic Charities and Islamic Relief for much of its humanitarian work. Our efforts are designed to help all mankind. No shipments are labeled 'For Latter-day Saints only.'"

- President Russell M. Nelson

We loaded on the bus for our next destination, one of the "most beautiful and peaceful locations in all the world," according to Uncle Buzzy.

Uncle Buzzy drove to a point where two white churches came into view. "The only remaining buildings from the early settlement of Kalawao are these two churches—the Siloama Congregationalist Church and the St. Philomena Catholic Church. In the early 1900s, the Hawaiʻi Board of Health began relocating patients from Kalawao to the Kalaupapa settlement. Not only was its climate warmer and drier, but it was also easier to access by sea. Because of these factors, the settlement of Kalawao was eventually completely abandoned, and everything moved to the Kalaupapa settlement three miles away on the western side of the peninsula. We'll most likely be the only people to come to Kalawao today."

Uncle Buzzy drove until the road came to an end at the edge of a small cliff. From the cliff, we could see an amazing view of the ocean as well as the northeast coastline of Moloka'i. We followed Uncle Buzzy down the steep incline on the southeast side of the road, traversing through trees and rocks until we came to a beach. Uncle Buzzy had us walk along the beach until we stood in the center of a cove. Out in the ocean, to our right, not far from the coastline, were two small islands, each about the size of several football fields with peaks rising from the water. On the south end of the cove was a large mountain range that rose from the coastline to the topside of Moloka'i. To the northwest of the cove was another mountain range. Both the mountains and the valley between them were lush and green.

As Manu and I took in the beauty and spirit of this place, Uncle Buzzy began speaking. "This cove is where some of the patients suffering from leprosy were dropped off. As I mentioned to you on the pier at Kalaupapa, Moloka'i can be an extremely difficult place to access by boat, and this cove can be even more problematic than the pier at Kalaupapa.

"In October 1881, the Warwick, the ship that usually transported leprosy patients to Moloka'i, was bringing twenty-two people to Kalawao. Father Damien and several residents stood on this very beach to greet them. The Warwick couldn't anchor due to stormy weather. The Kalawao residents attempted to bring whaleboats out to meet the Warwick, but the surf pounded them back to land. The captain of the Warwick ordered the patients thrown overboard, forcing them to attempt to swim ashore in the turbulent water.

"The residents of Kalawao and Father Damien rushed into the roaring surf to save the men, women, and children, who were struggling desperately for their lives in the waves. All twenty-two were pulled from the ocean, but two of the patients had taken in enough water that they were no longer breathing. They did all they could to revive these two patients, but to no avail. One of the patients died, cradled in the loving arms of Father Damien as he prayed and cried."[190]

Uncle Buzzy paused and we silently pondered this tragedy. I once again found myself in a state of shock and disbelief. It was hard to understand people acting with such disregard for the life of another. My feelings turned to sadness as I envisioned a drenched Father Damien sitting on this very beach with his head bowed and arms wrapped tightly around a patient in his lap, his body shaking as he wept.

After a few minutes of silence, Uncle Buzzy asked, "What lessons on ministry can we learn from this sad moment in history?"

My eyes drifted to the sand beneath my feet. My mind was still absorbed in the tragedies that so many people lived through. Looking toward Manu, I could see the light of teaching in his eyes.

"I believe," Manu answered, "that the Warwick captain must have viewed the leprosy patients as worthless cargo that he was delivering to this island to die. Whether they died at sea or at the settlement didn't matter to him. Father Damien had eyes to see. He saw past the disfigured faces and decaying bodies and saw a child of God with infinite worth and potential. Father Damien looked at those suffering from leprosy with the loving eyes of Jesus."

"Although I've told this story of the patient being thrown overboard many times, this in the first time I've had such a response. *Mahalo.*" Uncle Buzzy continued, "Manu, your comments bring to mind another story. Once a wealthy citizen of Honolulu sent a large gift of clothes to the colony. One of the visiting priests encouraged Father Damien not to give any of this clothing to patients who were unmarried and yet living together.[191] Father Damien rejected this idea and distributed the clothes to all who were in need, with no consideration of denomination, church attendance, or marital status. Father Damien was a father and servant to everyone in the peninsula, treating everyone equally. Father Damien built homes for Catholics, Protestants, Mormons, and those with no religious affiliation and he helped build churches on the peninsula for several denominations."[192]

I commented, "The Bible tells us that 'God is no respecter of persons.'[193] God doesn't treat a Baptist, Catholic, Evangelical, or Mormon differently. He treats them all the same. God doesn't see your denomination. God sees His child. Father Damien learned to see others as Jesus sees them."

Uncle Buzzy nodded in approval and said, "A Christlike minister sees others with the loving eyes of Jesus. Let's make our way back to the bus, and I'll take you to the St. Philomena Church."

CHAPTER 20

SAINT PHILOMENA CHURCH

"I would not be anywhere else for all the money in the world." [194]

- Father Damien

We climbed through the trees and back up the rocks to the bus and made the short drive to a cream-colored church with a green door. Surrounding the entire church property was a three-foot-high, dry-stack rock wall. The only entry into the property was a green, picket gate positioned directly in front of the church's double door entry. The peaceful splendor of the church grounds was magnificent. Through the coconut trees to the right of the church, you could see the ocean and the two small islands off of Kalawao cove. To the church's left was a dense group of trees that provided beauty and variety to the grounds.

Uncle Buzzy unlocked both the gate and the front door to the church, and we followed him inside. The small chapel was filled with wooden pews separated by a center aisle that spanned the entire length of the chapel. In front of each of the pews were rectangular holes about the size of a three-by-five-inch note card, which I found odd. After inviting us to sit in the front pew, Uncle Buzzy stood in front of us and asked, "What did Jesus do throughout his earthly ministry?"

"He ministered to the sick and taught His gospel," Manu answered.

Uncle Buzzy nodded his head in agreement. "Yes, Manu. Jesus Christ, our Master Teacher, healed men's souls by teaching them truth, the most important of which was that He came to redeem their souls from sin and death. This building is where Father Damien taught his sheep how to come to their Good Shepherd. During his ministry, Father Damien expanded this church three times as more and more people wanted to gather to worship and offer thanks to the Lord Jesus Christ. They gathered to hear the Word of God and to partake of the sacrament to receive the Lord's body and blood.

"Father Damien taught his flock that they were children of God with infinite worth and potential. He taught that death was merely a birth into a new world where pain and death were no more. He taught them the good news of Jesus Christ's victory over sin and death. He taught them Christ's words, which provided meaning for both their lives and their deaths. He kindled in their hearts the lively hope spoken of in the first epistle of Peter, 'Blessed be the God and Father of our Lord Jesus Christ, which according to his abundant mercy hath begotten us again unto a lively hope by the resurrection of Jesus Christ from the dead.'[195]

"Through both his teachings and by living Christ's gospel of unconditional love, Father Damien built a community of Aloha that was filled with a lively hope. When Father Damien arrived in

Kalaupapa, one of the nicknames of the settlement was 'the living graveyard.' With great satisfaction, Father Damien at one point wrote in a letter that this nickname was no longer applicable. He had transformed a settlement known for its lawlessness, neglect and despair into a community of respect, love, hope, and laughter."

"It's like Alma says," I interjected. "'And now, as the preaching of the word had a great tendency to lead the people to do that which was just—yea, it had had more powerful effect upon the minds of the people than the sword, or anything else, which had happened unto them—therefore Alma thought it was expedient that they should try the virtue of the word of God.'"[196]

"I love that scripture," Manu said. "The preaching of the Word will transform lives. The scriptures teach us that Jesus is the Word of God.[197] The preaching of the Word is the preaching of Jesus Christ. Nephi was taught by an angel that the iron rod in Lehi's vision of the tree of life was the word of God,[198] or in other words, the iron rod is Jesus Christ. We bring people to the iron rod of Jesus, and Jesus leads them to the fountain of living water and eternal life. When people take hold of the iron rod of Jesus, they will be changed for the better."

Uncle Buzzy replied with a smile. "I think you two are teaching me more than I'm teaching you. I've always been taught that in Lehi's vision the iron rod is the scriptures. I love the idea that the iron rod is the Lord Jesus Christ. We can learn from both Father Damien and Father Lehi that Christlike ministers teach the good news of the Lord Jesus Christ and bring people to Him."

There was a pause in the conversation and my eyes were drawn to the strange holes in the floor. "What's the purpose of these holes in the floor?"

"Good question, Elder Taylor," Uncle Buzzy said. "Father Damien noticed that during his sermons, several of the leprosy patients would gather outside by the open windows to watch and listen to the service. Although Father Damien invited them inside the church, they said they preferred to watch and listen from outside. Father Damien wanted to understand the motive behind this preference, so he inquired further. One of the many symptoms of leprosy was excess saliva. One patient summarized the dilemma best by saying, 'We can't sit through a service without spitting and we don't want to spit in the church.'

"After the service, Father Damien cut the holes you see in the church floor. With the aid of rolled up banana leaves, the patients would spit into these holes throughout Mass. While the world wanted to separate, quarantine, and isolate those suffering from leprosy, Father Damien was inclusive and found ways for those with leprosy to participate in activities they might otherwise have never been able to do.

"Before Father Damien came to Moloka'i, he served on the Big Island in Kohala for eight years. In fact, several members of his congregation from the Big Island became leprosy victims and were transported to Moloka'i. Before segregation became law, Father Damien had the opportunity to minister to men and women in the last stages of the disease. Despite his exposure to and experience with the disease, nothing could have prepared him for the heartbreaking conditions he would find when he arrived on Moloka'i.

"In a letter to his brother shortly after arriving in Kalaupapa,

Father Damien wrote of the conditions saying, 'Leprosy appears to be incurable. It eats away the flesh and as the flesh rots, it gives off a horrible smell. Even the breath of the leper is so foul that the air seems poisoned by it. It has been almost impossible for me to get used to the stench, and at Mass on Sunday, I felt I should have to leave the altar and go out into the fresh air, but I managed to control myself by thinking of Our Lord when He ordered them to open the grave of Lazarus in spite of Martha's words, 'Lord, by now he will smell.' But now I can go into the lepers' huts without reluctance, though there are times when I feel repelled by the open sores of the dying that are teeming with maggots. Pray that the Lord may bless my mission.'[199]

"Father Damien's superiors gave him clear instructions before he left for Moloka'i. He was told, 'Do not touch them. Do not allow them to touch you. Do not eat with them.'[200] Father Damien learned from his first day on Moloka'i that this would be impossible. Despite his aversion to the wounds and the putrid smells, he blessed the dying, he embraced the sick, and he ate with them from the same pot. Loving them meant letting go of an attitude of distance and instead being physically close to them.[201]

"A visitor to Kalawao who accompanied Father Damien on his daily visits recorded this account, 'Father Damien entered the hut to find two lepers lying on filth-encrusted mats, their bodies—such as was left of them—covered with blood and pus and with maggots swarming over their decaying flesh. The stench was almost tangible. He knelt beside them, washed and bandaged their sores, and comforted them with his words. He pulled biscuits and candy from his pocket for them. Father Damien bandaged the most revolting sores as if he were handling lovely flowers.'"202

Uncle Buzzy paused for a moment and asked, "What can we learn about ministry from these stories?"

The answer had been building in my heart the whole time I listened to Uncle Buzzy. The love Father Damien had for the people he served was still palpable in this place. "The Lord Jesus Christ frequently encountered those suffering from leprosy during His mortal ministry. He didn't avoid having physical contact with them. The Savior understood that those suffering from leprosy were starving for human touch, having been isolated and cast off from society. Christ didn't send these people away but instead brought them close. Jesus went out of His way to touch those suffering with leprosy. He touched them with hands filled with compassion, love, friendship, and healing. Father Damien did likewise."

As we spoke of the ministry of Father Damien and the Lord Jesus Christ, the Spirit filled the room.

Manu summarized the principle saying, "Christlike ministers are filled with compassion and are close to those they serve."

Uncle Buzzy began walking toward the door and said, "Please follow me. I'll show you the grounds surrounding the church."

We walked out the front doors and to the side of the church, stopping to stand between a group of headstones. "Around every church on the peninsula, you will find a graveyard," Uncle Buzzy explained. "During Father Damien's time in Kalaupapa, the population of the colony fluctuated between 700 and 1,100 patients, with new patients arriving and existing patients transitioning to the spirit world. Father Damien made daily visits to the sick, and he made regular visits to every home.

"Death was a frequent occurrence with approximately two hundred deaths each year. Journal entries like this one were common for Father Damien, 'I found one of my orphan girls dying. She had barely finished saying her prayers when she gave up her soul to the Lord. I made her coffin myself and dug her grave. After the funeral Mass this morning, I was informed of the death of two more of my Christians. That makes three burials today.'[203]

"Father Damien made sure there was a proper funeral service and burial for each person, holding multiple funerals each week. A missionary visiting Kalawao shared that while he was visiting, he was in the church alone when he heard music in the distance. As it grew nearer, he heard the resounding boom of a big drum, the rattle of kettledrums, and the sound of woodwind and brass. Father Damien, the coffin, and a large procession of people poured into the church.

"After the service, several women served as pallbearers. Two columns of women and girls followed the coffin. They were followed by the band and a large group of men and boys. The band played along the way and continued to play until the burial was complete. The missionary watched in awe at the care, love, and attention to detail during the funeral and burial. After the burial, the missionary asked Father Damien, 'Are all your funerals like this?' Father Damien answered, 'Always.'[204] With Father Damien, there were no mass funerals and no mass burials. The funerals and burials were done one by one."

Uncle Buzzy paused and said with a smile, "I think you know what question I'm going to ask now."

Manu answered, "You made this one easy. In fact, I think you already answered your own question. There is no mass ministry. Ministry is done one by one. The phrase 'one by one' is found throughout the scriptures when describing the Lord's ministry. When Christ appeared to those in America following His resurrection, the multitude went forth one by one to feel the prints of the nails in His hands and in His feet.[205] After teaching the people, Jesus healed the sick one by one and requested that the children be brought to Him. Jesus 'took their little children, one by one, and blessed them, and prayed unto the Father for them.'[206] After Jesus instituted the sacrament, 'he touched with his hands the disciples whom he had chosen, one by one, even until he had touched them all, and spake unto them as he touched them.'[207] If we want to serve as Christ did, we'll minister to individuals one by one."

We followed Uncle Buzzy as he walked to a grave near the side of the church. It was a simple grave marked with a black stone cross surrounded by a three-foot-high, black wrought iron fence. It was the grave of Father Damien. My breath caught in my throat to see the grave of a man who had done so much for so many. The simplicity of it seemed fitting for the humble servant he was.

Uncle Buzzy began, "I thought the grave of Father Damien would be an appropriate location for this story. There were several ministers throughout Hawai'i who were jealous and envious of the attention Father Damien was receiving. Several pastors wrote negative pieces on Father Damien to try and tarnish his good name. Whenever someone goes about doing good, the Devil will work to tear them down."

"Uncle Buzzy," I interjected, "this reminds me of a scripture in Helaman. It says, 'Satan did stir them up to do iniquity continually; yea, he did go about spreading rumors and contentions upon all the face of the land, that he might harden the hearts of the people against that which was good and against that which should come.'"[208]

Uncle Buzzy and Manu nodded in agreement. Uncle Buzzy continued, "Satan will use the universal sins of pride and envy to get people to spread rumors and lies. One of the pastors wrote that Father Damien was a dirty man, headstrong, and bigoted. In addition, he wrote that Father Damien was an impure man who had contracted leprosy because of sexual relationships with women in the settlement. The pastor's slanderous accusations, which had no merit or substance, were clearly false and driven by envy."

I could hardly imagine falsely accusing anyone of such things, but I wondered if it had hurt Father Damien because of the depth of the untruth. Here was a man trying to do good and caring for those cast off by the rest of the world and he was being criticized for it. I, too, had felt the sting of false accusations, though not of the same magnitude. I couldn't linger in my thoughts too long as Uncle Buzzy continued the story.

"A reporter went to Moloka'i after hearing the claims by the pastor. He interviewed many people in the Kalaupapa settlements and quickly found that Father Damien's actions bore witness of his goodness. His love and positive influence were immense. During his investigation, the reporter not only found no evidence to support the alleged accusations of the pastor, but when the reporter asked Father Damien to comment on the slanderous accusations made by the pastor, Father Damien simply replied, 'I forgive him wholeheartedly.'"[209]

"Wow," Manu said, "Father Damien was obviously a Christlike man. His response reminds me of Christ's response from the Cross. Jesus was slandered, spat upon, mocked, and nailed to the cross as an innocent man. After all the false accusation, hatred, and pain, Christ's first words from the cross were, 'Father, forgive them; for they know not what they do.'"[210]

Manu paused, flipping through his notebook. He stopped on a page and continued speaking. 'One of my favorite quotes from President Hinckley reads, 'A spirit of forgiveness and an attitude of love and compassion toward those who may have wronged us is the very essence of the gospel of Jesus Christ.'"[211]

"Thank you, Manu," I said. "As both you and Uncle Buzzy spoke, the Spirit pricked my heart and gently corrected me. I've had multiple occasions where people have spread rumors and lies about me. The hardest of these incidents was when the lies and rumors were spread by members of my ward and stake. I was deeply hurt. I felt a need to defend myself and correct the slander and lies that circulated. I felt resentment toward those who participated in the rumors. The Spirit has taught me there is a better way—the Christlike way. The only response I need to give to false accusations, rumors, criticism, and slander is the love and forgiveness that Father Damien and Jesus Christ both demonstrated."

Manu placed his arm around me and pulled me tightly to his side. "Elder Taylor, every evil you find in the world you will also find inside the Lord's church. However, it's more painful when it comes from within. Remember these words of the Savior, 'The servant is not greater than his lord. If they have persecuted me, they will also persecute you.'[212] Remember this promise of the Savior, 'Blessed are ye, when men shall revile you, and persecute you, and shall say all manner of evil against you falsely, for my sake. Rejoice, and be exceeding glad: for great is your reward in heaven: for so persecuted they the prophets which were before you.'[213] 'The Lord will fight for you; you need only to be still.'"[214]

The Spirit washed over me, and I was filled with the spirit of forgiveness and peace as I chose to put my trust in the power, promises, and blessings of the Lord.

Uncle Buzzy summarized our discussion, saying, "We can learn much about forgiveness from the lives of the Lord Jesus Christ and his servant, Father Damien. A Christlike minister is quick to forgive."

"Are you two ready to visit a new location?" Manu and I nodded our heads in unison. "We're going to head back to the city of Kalaupapa. At locations there, I'll share with you stories surrounding the death and burial of our friend, Father Damien."

CHAPTER 21

KALAUPAPA BOOKSTORE

"As a Latter-day Saint, you can accomplish the impossible. You can help shape the destiny of the human family! You can change the world. The Lord uses the unlikely to accomplish the impossible!" [215]

- President Russell M. Nelson

Father Damien, Age 33

As we loaded into the bus, Uncle Buzzy said, "I'm going to take you to meet my friend, Uncle Boogie, who runs the local bookstore. His given name is Clarence Kahilihiwa, but everyone calls him Uncle Boogie. He was diagnosed with leprosy when he was eight-years-old and was sent to Kalaupapa in 1959.

"The state of Hawaiʻi ended the practice of quarantining lepers to Molokaʻi in 1969 when a cure for leprosy became available. Although medical treatment stops the disease and removes the infection, it doesn't repair the damage done to the body. So, even though former patients like Uncle Boogie were healed of leprosy many decades ago, they still have the damage and disfigurement caused by the leprosy. Once treated and healed, they were free to leave Kalaupapa and live wherever they wanted. However, many residents chose to stay. This was their home, and they loved it here. Uncle Boogie was one of those who chose to stay.

"Between 1866 and 1969, eight thousand Hawaiians were sent to Kalaupapa. Uncle Boogie is one of only a dozen former patients still living in Kalaupapa. At the age of seventy-four, he is one of the youngest living former patients."

After a short three mile drive, we entered the city of Kalaupapa. Uncle Buzzy stopped at the stop signs in town, even though there were no other cars. If fact, not once during our visit to the peninsula did we see another car on the streets. Uncle Buzzy parked the bus in front of a small, well-kept building with dark green walls and white trim. It looked like a one-bedroom home with a small porch. We walked toward the building and the front door opened. Uncle Boogie flashed a big smile and called out, "Howzit, braddah?" as he made his way down the front steps.

Uncle Buzzy called back, "Howzit?"

Uncle Buzzy and Boogie embraced, and Boogie asked, "Who do you have with you today?"

"These are my friends, Manu and Elder Taylor," Uncle Buzzy replied.

Uncle Boogie inquired, "Elder Taylor, are you a Mormon missionary?"

"I was a missionary in Hawai'i twenty years ago, but Uncle

Buzzy and Manu continue to call me Elder Taylor."

"Well, if Elder Taylor is what Uncle Buzzy and Manu call you, that's good enough for me. Welcome to Kalaupapa, Elder Taylor," Uncle Boogie said, embracing me with a giant hug.

As we let go of one another, Uncle Boogie looked me in the eyes and said, "Well, you look young enough to still be a missionary, Elder Taylor."

"Yeah, I get that a lot, actually. Even after I had been home from my mission for years and had several children, I would still have workers at the Provo temple asking me where I was going on my mission."

After Uncle Boogie and Manu greeted one another with a hug, we followed Uncle Boogie up the steps onto the small porch and through the front door of the bookstore. We entered a small room lined with a few bookshelves that were filled with books related to Kalaupapa. On the walls were paintings and pictures of Father Damien and scenes from the peninsula and its history.

Uncle Buzzy turned to us and said, "There is a painting I would like to show you."

We followed Uncle Buzzy and stood in front of a painting of Father Damien.

"Near the end of Father Damien's life," Uncle Buzzy began, "an artist from England, Edward Clifford, came to paint a portrait of Father Damien. This is a copy of that painting."

Uncle Buzzy pulled out his notes and continued, "The painter stayed in the guesthouse near the Church of Saint Philomena. He had prepared himself for a stay in a wretched place of disease and devastation, but was moved by the cheerfulness and joy of living he experienced while visiting Moloka'i. While the artist painted at Father Damien's home, there were many visitors who came to see the progress of his paintings. The painter was struck by the happiness of the visitors. He was often surrounded by lively conversations and joyful laughter. The artist asked Father Damien numerous questions about his service in Moloka'i. He listened for hours to the stories of a man who he began to regard as a saint. Father Damien certainly didn't consider himself a saint, a martyr, or a hero. On the contrary, the artist wrote, 'a humbler man I never saw.'[216]

"Father Damien and Edward enjoyed their time together and became friends. Father Damien gave the artist a simple card with a drawing of flowers from the Holy Land with the handwritten note, 'To Edward Clifford, from his leper friend, Damien.' As Edward prepared to leave at the end of 1888, he asked Father Damien to sign his Bible. Father Damien wrote, 'I was sick and ye visited me.' Edward expressed his love to Father Damien and Father Damien reciprocated that love wholeheartedly.[217]

"George Woods, a medical officer for the United States Navy, reported after a visit to Kalaupapa, 'I have been to every country where there is leprosy, but I have never found a place where the lepers were so content and happy and where they had such good care taken of them as in this settlement.'"[218]

Smiling, I turned to Uncle Buzzy and said, "I'm guessing you're going to ask Manu and me what we learned about ministry from these stories."

"You're a quick student, Elder Taylor."

Uncle Boogie had a puzzled look on his face.

"Uncle Boogie, I'm giving Manu and Elder Taylor a special tour that we're calling, The Model of Ministry Tour."

"Never heard of it," Uncle Boogie replied.

"That's because it's the first time this tour has been given," Uncle Buzzy said chuckling. "We're just trying to learn from the example of Father Damien how to be a Christlike minister."

"Shoots," Uncle Boogie said, nodding his head in agreement. (In Hawai'i, shoots means cool or okay.)

"So, what have you two learned about ministry while we've been at the bookstore?" Uncle Buzzy inquired.

Manu was the first to answer. "The Savior frequently said to his followers, 'Be of good cheer.' I think an often-overlooked principle of ministry is laughter. A Hawaiian proverb says, 'One laughs when joyous.' A life in Christ should be a life of joy and laughter. The artist Edward Clifford talked about Father Damien's home being filled with laughter—evidence that Father Damien's home was a place of happiness and joy."

"Manu," I replied, "as you shared your comments, the Spirit brought a story to my mind. Recently, I received an invitation from Pastor Rick Warren to attend a three-day training for pastors at Saddleback Church in California. One of the breakout sessions I attended was given by a Catholic priest. This priest talked about how they transformed their sleepy parish into a thriving community of Christ. One of the comments he made really struck me. He said, 'When our Sunday service was boring, people thought God was boring.'"

Manu commented, "Elder Taylor, your story reminds me of this quote, 'Live so that others want to know Jesus because they know you.' If your life is filled with worry, stress, guilt, and sadness, will people want to emulate your life? Jesus Christ is the Holy One of Hope, the Prince of Peace, the Lord of Love, the High Priest of Happiness, the God of Grace, and the Rock of Rest. A life in Christ should be filled with joy."

Uncle Buzzy walked to a picture hanging on another wall. It was a black and white photo of youth with many different instruments. Pointing to the picture he said, "Father Damien established both a band and a choir in the colony. He used music to help those suffering to experience and express the joy of living." Uncle Buzzy referred to his notebook, "In one of his journal entries, he wrote, 'During Sunday High Mass my children sing like really great musicians.'"[219]

"When I think about the individuals who lived here, I'm filled with awe and respect," Manu commented with emotion. "They lived with joy and Aloha in very difficult circumstances."

Uncle Buzzy turned the pages of his notes and read, "A visitor to Kalaupapa shared this experience in 1876. 'I can never forget one summer, moonlit evening at Moloka'i when we went out after dinner and strolled up and down, enjoying the cool of the evening. We were attended by about a hundred lepers. A group of them had four drums and a dozen other instruments and for a couple of hours we were entertained by all kinds of music. Some of the players had only two or three fingers and their lips were grotesquely swollen or half-eaten away.'[220]

"Father Damien transformed a place filled with despair to a

place filled with joyful music. What principles of ministry do we learn from these stories?"

I answered, "A Christlike minister should laugh often and live with joy."

The others nodded in agreement. Uncle Boogie, with a huge smile on his face, exclaimed, "Kalaupapa is a happy place!"

His joyful exclamation caused all of us to laugh. They all laughed so easily and, when with them, so did I. I could think of so many back home who could use this kind of laughter.

"Uncle Boogie, may I show them the binder?" Uncle Buzzy asked.

Uncle Boogie laid a large, three-ring binder on one of the counters. Uncle Buzzy turned through the pages and stopped on a page with a color photograph of a beautiful ornate medallion.

"Here is the picture I was looking for," Uncle Buzzy said. "Princess Liliʻuokalani, who later became queen, visited Kalaupapa in 1881. As Liliʻuokalani came ashore, she was welcomed and greeted with a warm Aloha by eight hundred patients, dressed in their Sunday best. Father Damien accompanied the Princess over the dusty sand road that led from Kalaupapa to Kalawao. The princess toured the village, entering some of the neat, tiny white houses and visiting the boys' and girls' orphanages as well as the Protestant and the Catholic churches. Father Damien didn't want the princess to have to visit the hospital, but she insisted on going. She wasn't prepared for the sight of the swollen and mutilated faces of the lepers, looking at her from their small mats on the wooden floor. The princess exchanged smiles with a patient who only had one eye and had swollen earlobes that extended to his shoulders. The princess' eyes filled with tears as she spoke with a severely deformed and crippled girl.

"Just prior to Princess Lili'uokalani's departure, the girls' choir sang to her. They had prepared for weeks, excited for the princess' visit. When the girls finished, they looked toward the princess for her words of farewell.

"The princess rose and told the patients how proud she was of the courageous way they not only dealt with their illness, but also with being separated from their loved ones. Tears rolled down her cheeks and she couldn't speak for several minutes. After regaining her composure, she promised that the Kingdom of Hawai'i would do all it could to improve the living conditions in the colony.[221]

"The princess was again brought to tears as she watched those who had come with her on the steamer say goodbye to the loved ones they had come to visit. One mother cried as she hugged her badly disfigured child who had been exiled for three years. She knew she would never see him again. This mother stood on the steamer's deck, watching her son blow kisses to her until she was out of sight."[222]

Uncle Boogie noticed I was crying and handed me a box of tissues from behind the counter. I pulled a tissue from the box and wiped my eyes and nose.

"When Lili'uokalani returned to Honolulu," Uncle Buzzy continued, "she reported her experience. The patients and Father Damien made a deep impression on the Princess. She praised the efforts of the energetic Catholic priest to improve the lot of all of the exiles regardless of their religious convictions. The princess proposed Father Damien be honored with the title of Commander of the Royal

Order of Kalakaua, the highest honor in the kingdom.

"The royal family asked Bishop Hermann Koeckemann to personally deliver to Father Damien the medal, accompanied by a letter from Princess Liliʻuokalani. The entire colony gathered for the presentation ceremony, which included a large feast of roast pork, fresh fruit, and *poi*.

"While Father Damien was grateful for the support of the royal family, he wasn't concerned with titles and honors. In fact, he never wore his medal. At one point, a writer came to visit Father Damien and asked to see the medal. Father Damien declined, but the writer persisted and after several requests, Father Damien reluctantly retrieved the award for him to view. When Father Damien handed the writer the beautiful Moroccan case that contained the medal, the case was covered in a thick layer of dust. The writer clearly placed more value on this award than the man who had earned it."

Uncle Buzzy paused for a moment and asked, "What principles of ministry can we learn from this story?"

"The New Testament scripture 'God gives grace to the humble,'[223] comes to my mind," I replied.

"I was thinking along those same lines," said Manu. "A Christlike minister must be humble with an eye single to the glory of God."

Uncle Buzzy began turning the pages in the binder. He stopped on a page with a photograph of a book titled *The Lepers of Molokaʻi*. There was also a picture of the book's author, Charles Warren Stoddard.

Uncle Buzzy began, "American writer Charles Stoddard visited Father Damien in 1884. In his book, Charles gave this description of Father Damien, 'He was scarcely an elegant figure. His robe was stained and patched, his hair tousled like a schoolboy's, and his hands dirty and calloused with work, but his face shone with kindness and he had an infectious laugh.'"[224]

Manu commented, "Father Damien should give each of us hope that we can become a Christlike minister. He was an ordinary man with an extraordinary love. This should give us confidence. If you love like Father Damien did, you can do as much in your sphere of life as he did in his.[225] The path of ministry can be walked by everyone, regardless of who one is or where one lives."

"I recently read a great book by President Nelson called *Accomplishing the Impossible*," I said. "One of the themes throughout the book is that the Lord uses the simple, ordinary, and unlikely to accomplish the impossible."[226]

Manu replied, "We see God calling the unlikely throughout all scripture. In the New Testament, the apostle Paul recognized this pattern saying, 'Brothers and sisters, think of what you were when you were called. Not many of you were wise by human standards; not many were influential; not many were of noble birth. But God chose the foolish things of the world… God chose the weak things of the world… God chose the lowly things of this world and the despised things.'"[227]

"I was just thinking," I said, "that The Church of Jesus Christ of Latter-day Saints has used the slogan 'every member a missionary' for many years. I think an even better slogan would be 'every member a minister.'"

CHAPTER 22
MONUMENTS

"The political and journalistic world can boast of very few heroes who compare with Father Damien of Moloka'i."

- Mahatma Gandhi

Uncle Buzzy and Uncle Boogie showed us other pictures in the binder, and we enjoyed talking story together for some time. Uncle Buzzy eventually said, "I'm sad to say that it's time to leave. We still have one more stop to make before your tour is finished."

We each gave Uncle Boogie a hug and thanked him for his hospitality before we made our way back to the bus. "This next drive will be very short," Uncle Buzzy said.

After driving a couple of blocks, I stepped off the bus and immediately noticed a sign that read, "Mother Marianne Cope's Grave and Monument."

In the distance we could see a monument that was enclosed by a dry-stack rock wall. We followed a sidewalk, which led from the road to the gravesite area. Two eight-foot, white pillars that stood like sentinels on either side of the rock wall opening marked the entrance. The pillar on the right had a rock at its base with a hand-painted message that read, "Peace to all who enter here."

We quietly walked to the large, white monument that marked Mother Marianne's grave. The monument was unlike anything I had ever seen before: a statue of a saint and the Lord Jesus embracing one another while Christ was being crucified. The saint's arms were wrapped around the midsection of Christ. While Christ had one hand nailed to the cross, His other arm was free and wrapped around the shoulder area of the saint. The three of us stood in silence for some time, trying to take in this unique image.

Uncle Buzzy finally began speaking. "The mantle of Father Damien was taken up by the American sister, Marianne Cope. She arrived with a group of sisters on Moloka'i at the end of 1888, a few months before Father Damien's death. Their arrival was an enormous consolation to Father Damien and a fulfillment of his hopes and prayers.[228] Until her death in 1918, Mother Marianne and her fellow sisters dedicated themselves to those suffering from leprosy, with a special interest in the orphans.

"Another person who came to continue the work of Father Damien was Father Conrardy. Beginning in 1877, Father Conrardy and Father Damien kept a correspondence. When Father Conrardy learned that Father Damien was dying of leprosy and had no successor or fellow priest on Moloka'i, he offered to go. With Father Damien's help, Father Conrardy convinced the mission to allow him to go to Kalaupapa. He landed at the colony on May 17, 1888. He became Father Damien's fellow priest and dear friend during the last eleven months of his life, attending him on his deathbed and administering the last sacraments.[229]

"As Father Damien lay sick in bed nearing death, Father Conrardy and the Sisters asked Father Damien to leave his mantle to those continuing his ministry as the prophet Elijah had done with Elisha, so they could inherit his great heart for the lepers. With tear-filled eyes, Father Damien blessed Father Conrardy and the Sisters. Father Damien was relieved to know his friends would be well taken care of in his absence and said, 'Now, Lord, let your servant go in peace. The work for the lepers is in good hands; I am no longer needed.'"[230]

Uncle Buzzy paused and proceeded to walk to a large, red, granite monument that was topped by a giant cross, adjacent to Mother Marianne's monument. At the base of this monument was a profile image of Father Damien.

Uncle Buzzy continued, "While I've referred to Father Damien throughout our tour, he wasn't called by this name in Kalaupapa. When Father Damien arrived in Hawaiʻi, he became fluent in the language and culture of Hawaiʻi. He became one of them.

"The Hawaiian language consists of thirteen letters when you count the ʻokina. Since there is no letter "d" in the Hawaiian alphabet, Father Damien was given the name Kamiano. Father Damien lovingly called the members of the colony by their first names, and they lovingly called him Kamiano. While Kamiano is the Hawaiian rendering of Damien, I like to say that Kamiano is Hawaiian for true friend."

Uncle Buzzy began to tear up. He had spoken with emotion at several locations, but this was the first time I saw him cry. He pulled a handkerchief from his pocket and wiped his eyes and nose.

Flipping through his notes, he continued, "Several years after Kamiano's arrival on the peninsula, a visitor asked a group of leprosy patients if they were ever homesick. One of the lepers replied, 'I am happy here. I love Kamiano. He builds our houses. He cares for our every need. Even if I could, I would not want to leave if it meant being separated from my beloved Kamiano.'

"The feeling was mutual. Kamiano wrote his mother saying, 'I am very happy. Nothing in the world could induce me to leave.'[231]

"In the early 1880s, Father Damien suspected that he had contracted leprosy, but it wasn't until December 1884 that he knew this with confidence. After spending the evening making visits to homes throughout the settlement, he returned home feeling cold. He began preparing a basin of boiling water so he would be able to soak his feet in warm water before going to bed. Although he had a pitcher of cold water nearby that he intended to combine with the boiling water, he forgot to add the cold water to the mix.

"As he submerged his feet into the boiling water, he noticed that his feet were turning bright red, so he quickly pulled them from the water. He watched as blisters began to form on his feet and yet he felt no pain. There was no longer any doubt in his mind, for one of the sure signs of leprosy is the loss of feeling in your feet. A doctor paid a visit to Moloka'i shortly after this event and Father Damien asked him for an examination. The doctor found the bacilli of leprosy in the tissue from Father Damien's body and said, 'I'm afraid what you believe is true. You have leprosy.'

"In his first sermon on Moloka'i, Father Damien began with the phrase, 'We lepers.' He used this phrase repeatedly throughout his sermons during the next sixteen years. On the Sunday morning following his incident with the boiling water, Father Damien again began his sermon with the phrase, 'We lepers,' but this time the way he said 'we lepers' was different. The congregation understood that their beloved father and friend had contracted this terrible disease. His friends began to weep for him, for they knew intimately the pain and suffering he would have to endure.[232]

"Although the disease progressively disfigured Father Damien's face and limbs throughout the ensuing years, he physically remained remarkably strong and active. He served two parishes on his own, built new orphanages, and enlarged the church.[233]

"Father Damien continued to work and serve his beloved friends, despite his advancing symptoms. His ears became extremely swollen. His face, neck and hands were covered with tumors and swellings of all kinds. By 1888, Father Damien's health was rapidly deteriorating. On the 15th of October, Father Damien fell at the altar during High Mass. The debilitating effects of leprosy were taking their toll. Although Father Damien's body was plagued with many aliments, his pleasant mood and cheer remained. He continued taking care of the sick as if he were not sick. One visitor to Kalawao was surprised to find the dying Father Damien on the roof of the Church of Saint Philomena, coordinating the reconstruction work on the building and giving good-humored orders to those helping.[234]

"Father Damien was confined to his bed from March 28, 1889 until his death. Two priests were at his side during the final days of his life. One of these priests recorded Father Damien saying, 'All the wounds are closing, and the crust is turning black. This is the sign of imminent death. I am not mistaken, for I have seen many lepers die.' This same priest recorded, 'He is prepared for death. It was truly edifying to see him. He seemed so happy. He was bright and cheerful, as usual.'

"Mother Marianne, Sisters Leopoldina and Vincentia, the nuns who had taken over care of the girls' orphanage for Father Damien, came with a group of orphan girls to visit Father Damien on his deathbed. At the conclusion of their visit, Father Damien said to his girls, 'I shall die soon, my children, but you will not be left alone. These sisters will care for you and you are now going with them to Kalaupapa.' The girls sobbed as if their hearts would break. All but two went with the sisters. These two little girls knelt and clutched Kamiano's legs, crying, 'Father, we are going to stay with you until you die.' They were allowed to remain, and they stayed with him until he went to heaven.[235] Father Damien gave them the gifts of love and friendship, and in return he received great love and friendship. By giving, he received.

"Father Damien's final, brief letter was addressed to the settlement's resident physician, Doctor Swift. He wrote, 'Jobo Puhomamia is spitting blood. Please spare a moment to go and see him. Please do this favor for your friend.'

"While on the cross, Jesus thought of the welfare of His mother, His friends, His executors, and those executed with Him. Father Damien's death was an example of the Master he served. Until the end, Father Damien's thoughts went to caring for his friends.[236]

"On the day after Palm Sunday, Father Damien knew his entry to heaven had come. He offered these final words, 'The Lord is calling me to celebrate Easter with him.'[237] Father Damien died at 8:00 a.m. on Monday, April 15, 1889, at the age of forty-nine."

Uncle Buzzy paused to wipe his eyes and blow his nose, and Manu and I did the same. The Spirit was powerful. We were all brought to tears as we experienced the final moments of Saint Damien's life.

Uncle Buzzy continued, "In his last letter to his brother, Father Damien wrote, 'I am happy and content, and though seriously ill, I desire nothing else than the fulfillment of the holy will of the good God. I am being gently dragged toward the grave. May the good God strengthen me and grant me the grace of perseverance and a good death.'[238]

"Father Damien fulfilled his desire for a good death. He provided both an example of how to live and how to die. He died in the arms of Father Conrardy and Brother Sinnett. Brother Sinnett wrote of Father Damien's passing, 'I have never seen a happier death.'[239]

"Father Damien's body was taken to the church. His body was prayed and wept over by his friends until the funeral the next day. It was a funeral like the hundreds conducted each year. Father Damien saw the death of more than two thousand of his friends during his sixteen years on Moloka'i. The whole settlement participated in the funeral Mass and the procession to the cemetery.

"The cross bearer was first in the procession, leading with the symbol of an empty cross—a reminder of the Lord's triumph over sin and death and His gift of a glorious resurrection. A large group of musicians followed, playing with great vigor. The sisters, women, and girls of the settlement followed the band. The casket followed the women and was carried by eight pallbearers dressed in white. The coffin was followed by the men and boys. A grave had been dug for Father Damien at the foot of the giant *pū hala* tree. Father Damien was laid to rest under the same tree where he first slept upon his arrival at Kalawao."

Uncle Buzzy paused again to wipe his eyes and nose with his handkerchief. He pointed to the scripture engraved on the base of the monument, John 15:13, and said, "Elder Taylor, will you please read this."

I began, "Greater love hath no man than this, that a man lay down his life for his friends."

As I read this scripture, the Spirit consumed my entire being. We stood in silence, enjoying the fruits of the Spirit.[240] None dared speak for the sacredness of the moment—warmth and peace filled my soul.

After a period of silence, Uncle Buzzy asked, "What principles of ministry do we learn from these stories?"

Manu opened his mouth and it was filled by the Spirit, "When serving as a minister of the Lord Jesus Christ, there is no more important title than that of friend."

"I agree, Manu," I said. "Father Damien saw the fulfilment of the Savior's promise, 'Whoever loses his life for my sake will find it.'[241] In giving his life, he found his life. His service to others made him 'the happiest missionary in the world.'"[242]

Manu commented, "The Lord declares in the Doctrine and Covenants, 'I will give unto you a pattern in all things.'[243] The ministry of the Lord Jesus Christ and the ministry of Father Damien provide us with a pattern to follow. The life of Father Damien can help each us be more Christlike ministers. The holiness of one person inspires holiness in others."[244]

"Manu, that makes me think of a quote I once read," Uncle Buzzy said. "In a letter, the Anglican priest, Hugh B. Chapman, wrote to Damien. He said, 'You have taught me more by the story of your life than all the commentaries I have ever read.'"[245]

"That's a beautiful quote," Manu said. "Father Damien provides us an example of what's most needed today: love in action—a vigorous, outgoing, tireless, and self-sacrificing love. To abandon yourself to such a love is dangerous, but it will give you true happiness. To transform your home and community to a place of laughter, hope, love, kindness, and joy, you just have to love and serve your family and community as did Father Damien. You don't have to be exiled to Kalaupapa to change the world. You just have to minister to those in your home, congregation, and neighborhood. To be a mighty minister of the Lord Jesus Christ, you just have to love and serve."

Uncle Buzzy nodded his head in agreement and said, "Father Damien showed us how to live Aloha."

We walked in silence back to the bus. As we took our seats, Uncle Buzzy said, "There is much more I would like to show you, but it's time to return to the topside."

I was saddened to be leaving but was grateful for the opportunity to spend time in Kalawao and Kalaupapa. As we drove back to get our mules, I asked, "I read that Father Damien was made a Saint by the Catholic Church. Is that correct?"

"Father Damien was canonized by Pope Benedict XVI in 2009,"

Uncle Buzzy replied. "He is the first Catholic saint from Hawai'i, but his ministry and example extends far beyond Hawai'i and Catholicism. His example of Aloha, unconditional love, and service has inspired people of all denominations and faiths. He isn't just a saint for Hawai'i; he is a saint for the world. He isn't just a saint for the Catholics; he is a saint for all of us. In a celebrity-driven age, with heroes coming from the worlds of sports, movies, music, and politics, there is a great need for heroes like Saint Damien. Although I think his status as a saint is important in providing an example for the world to emulate, I still think of him as Kamiano—my friend."

Uncle Buzzy pulled the bus to a stop. We exited the bus, mounted our mules, and began riding along the shore of the ocean. "Uncle," I said, "you promised that I would be forever changed as a result of my trip to Kalaupapa, and you were correct."

Uncle Buzzy smiled and replied, "Our tour today was a miracle. There is no question that the Lord was guiding our travels and discussion."

"Elder Taylor, Uncle Buzzy is a child of light," Manu said. "With each visitor, he shares his light, the light of Moloka'i, and the light of Father Damien. Sharing light is like one candle lighting another candle. The first candle loses nothing by lighting another candle. The world just becomes a little brighter for both."

In my mind I saw the image of a world globe with thousands of dots of light radiating from it. Uncle Buzzy, a man of light from the small town of Ho'olehua, loved and shared light with a few people on each tour and in so doing, had brightened the world. I was excited to share the light I had been given with my family and friends in Idaho.

As we made our way up the trail, Uncle Buzzy whistled elaborate tunes. The ride up the sea cliffs was much more comfortable than the ride down since it was much easier to lean back on the mule during the steep climb than leaning forward during the descent.

We helped Uncle Buzzy care for the mules when we arrived back at the stable. After the mules were settled, we exchanged hugs and goodbyes with Uncle Buzzy.

As we were heading out, Uncle Buzzy exclaimed, "Wait! I almost forgot to give you your certificates." He pulled two certificates from a drawer. He wrote in our names, the names of our mules, and signed his name on the signature line. He placed a circle stamp on the certificate that contained the date and the text, "Kalaupapa National Historical Park—Kalaupapa Mule Tour."

Uncle Buzzy handed us our certificates. I read mine aloud. "Be it known that Elder Taylor was a member of this expedition on the 'World-Famous Kalaupapa Trail' of Molokaʻi, Hawaiʻi, and having faced the obstacles, precipices, and hazards of this treacherous trail and endured the vicissitudes of the narrow passage between rim and destination while bearing the caprices of the long-eared mount named Alika, is now an acknowledged member of the renowned Aliʻi Mule Skinners of Molokaʻi, Hawaiʻi, and is endowed with all the rights and privileges that are bestowed upon the members of this select and accomplished fraternity."

"*Mahalo*, Uncle Buzzy. This will be a cherished memento," I said.

"You're welcome, Elder Taylor. May it always serve as a reminder of our experience together today," Uncle Buzzy replied.

Manu and I returned to the car and began the ninety-minute drive back to Naniwaiwai's home. About thirty minutes into our drive, Manu pulled off to the side of the road by a small church. There was a sign nearby that read, "Saint Joseph Church—Kamalo—Built by Saint Damien in 1876."

We parked the car and walked toward the church. As we walked, Manu said, "Father Damien also served those who lived on the topside of Moloka'i. This is one of the churches he built."

The white, well-kept church was surrounded by a dark, dry-stack rock wall. As was the case with the other older churches we visited, there was a cemetery on the church grounds. A statue of Father Damien stood to the right of the church. The statue, which was an accurate representation of Father Damien's actual size, depicted him standing with his arms together in front of him, holding a walking stick.

As we approached the statue, I felt like I knew Father Damien. I loved and respected him and wanted to express my gratitude to this giant of a man in some way. I took the flower lei that Uncle Buzzy had given me and placed it around the neck of Father Damien. As I looked into his eyes I said, "Aloha, my brother. Thank you for your example of faith, love, compassion, and service. I will be a better minister of the Lord Jesus Christ because of your Christlike example. *Mahalo*, my friend. I look forward to meeting you in heaven."

Manu took his lei from around his neck and placed it around the neck of Father Damien and said, "I love you, brother."

This act of placing the leis around Father Damien's neck and expressing our gratitude and love to him seemed a fitting end to our

Model of Ministry tour.

As we continued our drive to Hālawa Valley, Manu asked, "Elder Taylor, why do we erect monuments and statues?"

Manu's question surprised me. It seemed like a simple question and yet, I really didn't have a good answer. "I've actually never given that question any thought," I said. "So, I don't know what to say." Manu smiled but remained silent for a minute while I pondered.

"Thank you for your honesty and humility, Elder Taylor," Manu said reassuringly. "We should never feel foolish about not knowing an answer to something or feel that our opinions aren't adequate if they aren't profound or articulated well. Saying, 'I don't know' is one of the most intelligent and courageous responses a person can ever speak."

"Thank you, brother."

"I think years ago, the reason for monuments used to be very clear," Manu began, "but their true purpose has been lost over time. Honoring exceptional individuals is certainly an outcome of monuments, but it's not their true objective. Honoring others is a passive activity since we are simply focusing on the greatness found in another person. The true intent of monuments is active, not passive. Monuments are built to inspire us to be our best selves.

"When we erect a monument, we are reminded of the love, service, courage, and faith that lies within each of us as children of an all-powerful God. Monuments provide a light in the darkness. They show us examples of truth in action. They provide heroes for us to look to and ensure that the stories of these heroes are not forgotten but are told from generation to generation. When a hero's story is forgotten, that hero and the great truths his or her life taught us are lost, and that's a tragedy.

"As stories of Father Damien's service spread throughout the world, thousands donated to help those exiled to Kalaupapa. Not only did the leper colony on Kalaupapa receive help, but so did organizations that assisted those suffering from leprosy in other communities. They received greater support through both volunteers and donations. Many new organizations were founded, many of them bearing Father Damien's name, to assist the poor, sick, and orphaned. Countless individuals were inspired to a life of full-time ministry and service.

"It's now one hundred and twenty-seven years since Father Damien went to heaven, but he continues to inspire people throughout the world every day because of the monuments and statues that have preserved and perpetuated his story. It's simply impossible to calculate the number of people who have been inspired to live better lives because of Father Damien's example.

"That number has increased by one after today," I said. "Learning about Father Damien's life has touched me in a profound way. I've already been thinking of changes I want to make and ways I want to serve God with my particular gifts and talents."

"As have I, Elder Taylor, as have I," Manu said. "Monuments are built to increase our faith in the Lord Jesus Christ, who is the source of all power, strength, and goodness. Monuments provide heroes who exhibited Christlike qualities and who inspire us, teach us, and show us a more excellent way to live. Monuments plant within us the seed of desire to emulate Jesus Christ.

"Elder Taylor, will you please get out your scriptures and read Joshua chapter four?"

"Sure," I said.

As I removed my scriptures from their case and looked for the reference, Manu said, "In Joshua chapter three, we read about the miracle of the children of Israel crossing over the Jordan River. As they stepped into the water, the Lord stopped the river and dried the soil. Israel walked across the Jordan on firm ground. In chapter four, the Lord told Joshua to create a monument of twelve stones. This monument was erected so the miracle of the Jordan crossing would be told from generation to generation. Please read verses twenty-one to twenty-four."

I began to read, "'And he spake unto the children of Israel, saying, When your children shall ask their fathers in time to come, saying, What mean these stones? Then ye shall let your children know, saying, Israel came over this Jordan on dry land. For the Lord your God dried up the waters of Jordan from before you, until ye were passed over, as the Lord your God did to the Red sea, which he dried up from before us, until we were gone over: That all the people of the earth might know the hand of the Lord, that it is mighty.'"[246]

Grinning from ear to ear, Manu said, "Why do we build monuments? 'That all the people of the earth might know the hand of the Lord, that it is mighty.'"

CHAPTER 23
FAMILY REUNION

"Be the children of light." [247]

- Jesus Christ

Tuesday was the day of the family reunion. We spent the morning helping Naniwaiwai with preparations for the event and then made our way to Hālawa Beach Park around noon. The reunion officially began with *pule* (prayer), but it wasn't like the typical prayer offered at the beginning of a ward party. One of the family *kupuna* offered an *oli* (chant) in Hawaiian, asking for God's blessings on the gathering and inviting all ancestors to come and share in the celebration.

The prayer touched my heart as now the family reunion's attendance would include members of the family who were no longer living on the earth. It made perfect sense, though. Why wouldn't deceased family members want to be invited to their family reunion? Even if they no longer had a physical body, they were still very much a part of the family.

Food, music, hula, and chants filled the day. Numerous stations run by aunties and uncles lined the park. These stations provided family members the opportunity to participate in making leis, weaving, quilting, kapa making, kapa art, and woodcarvings. Family chants and dances were performed throughout the reunion, and family genealogy charts encircled the pavilion, showing family lines and where each person and place related to the whole.

At one point during the reunion, Naniwaiwai took the stage. The family gathered around, closely forming a circle around her.

She held a bowl in the air and said, "It's time to present the Bowl of Light Award. [248] As you know, we present this award at each family reunion to a family member who has brought light to our family—an individual who is an example of light and who brings honor to our family name." After summarizing the bowl of light story, Naniwaiwai shared stories about past recipients of the award.

Naniwaiwai then said, "Before we present the award this year, we must first perform another ceremony. Elder Taylor, will you please join me in the circle?"

I looked at her in confusion. I wasn't sure what her plan was, but it definitely wasn't something she had discussed with me beforehand. Several members of the family gave each other knowing glances. A flutter of nerves went through my stomach.

Once I was standing next to her, she turned to me and said, "As we met as a family to discuss the nominations for this year's Bowl of Light Award, your name was presented. As we discussed your nomination, one of the *kupuna* said, 'I think Elder Taylor is deserving of the award, but the award has always gone to a member of our family.' Another *kupuna* quickly replied, 'This is an easy problem to solve. Elder Taylor has become one of us—he thinks like us and understands our ways—let's *hānai* him and make him an official member of our family.'

"Elder Taylor, *hānai* is the Hawaiian practice of adoption that has been performed by our people for many centuries. Our family is filled with excitement at the prospect of your becoming part of our *'ohana*. Would you like to officially be a part of our family?"

Tears began to well up in my eyes. I was overwhelmed by their love, hospitality, generosity, friendship, and acceptance. I loved these people and felt privileged to know them and to be loved by them.

I answered, "I can think of no greater honor than to be joined with this *'ohana*. I promise to do my best to bring light and honor to our family name." Clapping and a few happy cheers from the other family members made me laugh and stopped the tears from falling.

Naniwaiwai quieted them with a stare. "Now that you're Hawaiian, Elder Taylor, you will need a Hawaiian name. This assignment was given to me. After pondering extensively on what your new name should be, your name was revealed to me in a dream. Your new name is 'Alohi. 'Alohi means to shine, sparkle, and glitter; to be bright, brilliant, and splendid. You are 'Alohi. You're a light that shines, sparkles and glitters. You're bright, brilliant, and full of splendor. You are 'Alohi."

The family converged together closely for a group hug and began to joyously chant, "'*Ohana!*"

I couldn't speak or make a sound. How could I ever express my gratitude and love to such a welcoming people? All I could do was let the tears fall. There was more laughter and I laughed with them. More than anything, I wanted to share this experience with my wife and children. I was excited to bring them to Moloka'i to meet their new aunties, uncles, and cousins.

The family formed a circle with Naniwaiwai and me at the center. I wiped the tears from my eyes and with a smile on my face, I said, "Whenever I fill out a form that requires you to state your ethnicity, I check the box Pacific-Islander. Now, it's official."

Laughter erupted throughout the family circle. When the laughter subsided, Naniwaiwai continued, "'Alohi, my son. I would like to present to you the Bowl of Light Award."

There were clapping and cheers as Naniwaiwai handed me the handmade wooden bowl. I rotated the bowl in my hand, captivated by its beauty and design. On one side of the bowl was carved the question, *"pehea ka lā?"* On the bottom of the bowl was carved "'Be the children of light.' John 12:36."

Naniwaiwai stepped back and joined the rest of the family in the circle, leaving me alone in the center. It was my turn to speak. The Spirit whispered, "Chant the family genealogy. Open your mouth and it will be filled."

After receiving Naniwaiwai's handwritten papers of her genealogy chant, I had felt a strong desire to learn the chant. I had spent time each evening and morning memorizing and practicing it. I didn't understand at the time why it was so important to learn the family chant, but I understood now. The eyes of each family member were fixed upon me as I opened my mouth and began the *oli* of the family genealogy. I could feel myself being filled with *mana* from my new ancestors and was given the gift of tongues as I chanted. At the conclusion of the *oli*, I said, *"Aloha au iā 'oe."* ("I love you.")

The family converged on me once again for another large *ʻohana* hug and then returned to forming a circle around me. One of the family *kupuna* joined me in the circle and said, "ʻAlohi, you have a gift to see with spiritual eyes. You see much more than the beaches and the palm trees. You see the real beauty of Molokaʻi—the beauty of Aloha—the beauty of *ʻohana.* *ʻAhuwale ka nane hūnā* is a Hawaiian phrase, which in English would be, 'The hidden meaning is seen.' You have the gift to write and teach in a way that others can see the divine truths of Aloha—truths that are not new but are merely hidden and in need of rediscovery. It's your *kuleana* to illuminate the way of Aloha, which is the way of Zion. This is the way to ready a people to welcome the Lord for His millennial reign. Our *ʻaumākua* (guardian angels) are now your *ʻaumākua.* They will help you with your *kuleana* just as they help each of us with ours."

CHAPTER 24

FLIGHT HOME

"Hawai'i will change you if you will let it."

- Hawaiian Kupuna

The next morning my emotions swirled and battled within me. In a few hours, I would be boarding a flight to Idaho. The prospect of seeing my wife and children filled me with joy. I'd missed them dearly, and there was so much I wanted to share with them. I was filled with sorrow, though, at the thought of leaving my new 'ohana.

As Manu and I prepared to depart for the airport, Naniwaiwai gave me a big hug. "Elder Taylor," she said, "you are now my son, and I want to see my daughter and grandchildren. Please return soon with your wife and children."

"Of course, Naniwaiwai," I said. "I'm always looking for reasons to return to Hawai'i." We embraced once more. "I love you, Naniwaiwai," I said. "I love you, too, 'Alohi," she replied.

Manu and Naniwaiwai then embraced, exchanging, "*Aloha au iā 'oe*" with one another.

As Manu and I began our drive to the airport, I felt impressed to share with Manu an email that I had received the day before from a reader of *The Way of Aloha: Lana'i*.

"Manu, I said, "I feel impressed to share an email with you that I received yesterday."

Manu replied, "Wonderful. I would love to hear it."

I pulled out my phone and began to read the email, "Aloha! I just finished reading *The Way of Aloha: Lana'i* for the second time. It is such an amazing book and has brought such a great spirit into my life. Many of my friends and neighbors have noticed a change in me that I attribute to your book. They have now gone out and bought the book so they can experience its message for themselves. I'm looking forward to the next books in the series. Mahalo! Melinda."

"Elder Taylor, it has been wonderful to see the positive impact your book has had on people's lives. Your book is a powerful tool to share the good news of Jesus Christ. The good news of Jesus Christ is much more than information. It is transformation. Melinda was changed as she received the good news of Jesus Christ. 2 Corinthians 5:17 says, 'If any man be in Christ, he is a new creature.' The Master Jesus Christ not only cleanses us from sin, but He also transforms our way of thinking and acting so that we become more like Him. Elder Taylor, would you mind turning to John chapter two?"

"Not at all," I replied. "What verse do you want me to start with?" I asked.

"The first verse will be good, Elder Taylor."

"'And the third day there was a marriage in Cana of Galilee; and the mother of Jesus was there: And both Jesus was called, and his disciples, to the marriage. And when they wanted wine, the mother of Jesus saith unto him, They have no wine. Jesus saith unto her, Woman, what have I to do with thee? mine hour is not yet come. His mother saith unto the servants, Whatsoever he saith unto you, do it. And there were set there six water pots of stone, after the manner of the purifying of the Jews, containing two or three firkins apiece. Jesus saith unto them, Fill the water pots with water. And they filled them up to the brim. And he saith unto them, Draw out now, and bear unto the governor of the feast. And they bare it. When the ruler of the feast had tasted the water that was made wine, and knew not whence it was: (but the servants which drew the water knew;) the governor of the feast called the bridegroom, And saith unto him, Every man at the beginning doth set forth good wine; and when men have well drunk, then that which is worse: but thou hast kept the good wine until now.'"[249]

"You can stop there, Elder Taylor," Manu said. "Turning water into wine is the first recorded miracle of Jesus. There is a common element in each of Christ's miracles—transformation. Transformation comes as we put our faith and trust in the Lord Jesus Christ. The water was transformed to wine because of the faith of His mother. She showed her trust in the Lord when she said, 'Whatsoever he saith unto you, do it.'

"We show our faith and trust in the Lord when we ask, 'Lord, what would you have me do?' and then have the faith to do whatever He commands. When you trust your life to Christ, your life will be transformed, just as the water was transformed into wine."

As I listened to Manu's wisdom, it was hard not to be sad, knowing that my time with him was soon coming to a close. Mostly, though, I was filled with gratitude for the time I had been given this week to be taught by the Holy Spirit through this good man. It was a blessing to have been with Manu again, even if only for a short time.

Our drive ended much too quickly. We returned our rental car and made the short walk to the small terminal to wait for our flights. We talked story as we waited for our time to board. I was to depart first. Manu stood up to embrace me as I got up to leave.

"I love you, brother," I said.

"I love you too, brother," Manu replied. "Now let's make sure we don't go another twenty years before we get together again."

Smiling, I replied, "I have a feeling we're going to be meeting together often. The Spirit brought us together twenty years ago on Lanaʻi, and the Spirit brought us together again this week on Molokaʻi. I believe this trip is just the beginning of our adventures together."

Manu nodded in agreement.

I walked toward the door, but turned to say, "*A hui ho*, Manu."

"*A hui ho*, Elder Taylor," Manu replied.

There were no long lines or jet ways here. Just a normal door, which exited to the outside, leading to a short walk to a small airplane.

As I walked out the door, enveloped by the beautiful Hawaiian weather, I raised my hands and head toward heaven and shouted, "Praise the Lord for the Lord is good."[250]

In response, I heard the shout of Manu fill the terminal, "*Hoʻomaikaʻi i ke Akua!*"[251]

I was a different person boarding the plane home. After just a week with the people and places of Molokaʻi, I had been changed. The words from the first sign I saw on the island flashed into my mind, "Don't change Molokaʻi. Let Molokaʻi change you." This was more than a message. It was a prophecy, and the prophecy was fulfilled. I had been forever changed for the better because I was blessed to live for a few days among the sacred people and places of Molokaʻi.

EPILOGUE

"The world will turn to Hawai'i as they search for world peace because Hawai'i has the key...and that key is Aloha."

- Aunty Pilahi Paki

This is the second book in *The Way of Aloha* series. The first book in the series is called *The Way of Aloha: Lanaʻi*. Future books will take place on other Hawaiian islands, where we will visit historical and sacred locations on these islands and explore additional truths and principles from ancient Hawaiʻi. Future books in the series will include:

The Way of Aloha: Oʻahu
The Way of Aloha: Maui
The Way of Aloha: The Big Island
The Way of Aloha: Kauaʻi

I hope you enjoyed this book. I would love to hear from you. Please email me at: Aloha@CameronCTaylor.com

ACKNOWLEDGEMENTS

I would like to thank the many people who helped with the completion of this book. I would like to express individual thanks:

To the people of Molokai for their work to preserve and protect their island and culture. God is with you in your efforts. Mahalo nui loa for your hospitality, friendship, and generosity.

To Paula Taylor. I am greatly blessed to be married to Paula. She is a woman of many, many talents. She has played a key role in the writing and editing of each of my books. I appreciate her constant and enduring support. She is a super hero.

To Todd Thompson for the cover art and book design. Todd is a brilliant designer and is a joy to work with.

To Amanda Brown, Stacey Nash, Camille Gregory, and Janis Bowers for their work as editors.

ABOUT THE AUTHOR

Cameron C. Taylor is a best-selling author of more than ten books. His books have been endorsed by Richard Paul Evans, Dr. Stephen R. Covey, Jon Huntsman, Sr., Susan Easton Black, Lou Holtz, Ken Blanchard, and many others. Cameron graduated with honors from Brigham Young University. He developed a passion for the history and culture of Hawai'i while serving there as a full-time missionary. Cameron lives in Idaho with his wife and their four children.

Aloha@CameronCTaylor.com
www.CameronCTaylor.com

ENDNOTES

1   Pali Jae Lee and Koko Willis, *Tales from the Night Rainbow* (Night Rainbow Publishing Co., 1990), 78.

2   Exodus 20:13, Jubilee Bible 2000.

3   Matthew 13:16, King James Version.

4   Philippians 4:13, New King James Version.

5   Doctrine and Covenants 124:1.

6   Doctrine and Covenants 35:13.

7   Doctrine and Covenants 133:58.

8   Russell M. Nelson, *Accomplishing the Impossible* (Salt Lake City, UT: Deseret Book, 2015), 1-12.

9   Bruce Wilkinson, *Beyond Jabez* (Sister, OR: Multnomah Publishers, 2005), 108.

10   Acts 10:38.

11   Malcom Nāea Chun, *No Nā Mamo* (Honolulu, HI: University of Hawai'i Press), 45, 41.

12   1 John 4:8, New Living Translation.

13   Oliver Cowdery, *Messenger and Advocate*, October 1835, 198.

14   Doctrine and Covenants 84:88.

15   Van James, *Ancient Sites of Maui, Moloka'i, and Lāna'i* (Honolulu, HI: Mutual Publishing, 2001), 124.

16   Charles R. Swindoll, *Growing Strong in the Seasons of Life* (Grand Rapids, MI: Zondervan, 1994), 427.

17   C.S. Lewis, *Mere Christianity* (Grand Rapids, MI: Zondervan, 2001), 82.

18   Acts 10:38.

19   Colossians 3:23, New International Version.

20   Matthew 18:20.

21   3 Nephi 17:5.

22   3 Nephi 17:21-22.

23   Thomas S. Monson, "God's Gifts to Polynesia's People," *General Conference*, October 1966.

24   Matthew 11:28.

25   Genesis 7:2.

26   John 20:19-22.

27   Jack Canfield, Mark Victor Hansen, Sharon Linnea, Robin Rohr, *Chicken Soup from the Soul of Hawai'i* (Deerfield Beach, FL: Health Communication, Inc.), 164.

28   3 Nephi 17:17.

29   "For then will I turn to the people a pure language, that they may all call upon the name of the Lord, to serve him with one consent." Zephaniah 3:9.

30   Ben Behunin, *Remembering Isaac: The Wise and Joyful Potter of Niederbipp* (Abendmahl Press, 2009), 18-19.

31   2 Nephi 10:21.

32   Doctrine and Covenants 133:20.

33   Doctrine and Covenants 89:18.

34   Job 40:16.

35   Pali Jae Lee and Koko Willis, *Tales from the Night Rainbow* (Night Rainbow Publishing Co., 1990), 18-19.

36   3 Nephi 17:6-7.

37   President Russell M. Nelson, "The Price of Priesthood Power," *General Conference*, April 2016.

38   Van James, *Ancient Sites of Maui, Molokaʻi, and Lānaʻi* (Honolulu, HI: Mutual Publishing, 2001), 127.

39   R. Lanier Britsch, *Unto the Islands of the Sea: A History of the Latter-day Saints in the Pacific* (Salt Lake City: Deseret Book, 1986), 97-98.

40   William A. Cole and Edwin W. Jensen, *Israel in the Pacific: A Genealogical Text for Polynesia* (Salt Lake City: Genealogical Society of Utah, 1961), 384.

41   Mark E. Petersen, "New Evidence for the Book of Mormon," *Improvement Era* (June 1962) 65:456–459; also in *Conference Report* (April 1962) 111–115.

42   "The Dedicatory Prayer in the Hawaiian Temple," *Improvement Era*, February 1920, 283.

43   "And other sheep I have, which are not of this fold: them also I must bring, and they shall hear my voice; and there shall be one fold, and one shepherd." John 10:16.

44   "And verily, verily, I say unto you that I have other sheep, which are not of this land, neither of the land of Jerusalem, neither in any parts of that land round about whither I have been to minister. For they of whom I speak are they who have not as yet heard my voice; neither have I at any time manifested myself unto them. But I have received a commandment of the Father that I shall go unto them, and that they shall hear my voice, and shall be numbered among my sheep, that there may be one fold and one shepherd; therefore I go to show myself unto them." 3 Nephi 16:1-3.

45   2 Nephi 29:12, 11.

46   Pali Jae Lee and Koko Willis, *Tales from the Night Rainbow* (Night Rainbow Publishing Co., 1990), 23.

47   Doctrine and Covenant 133:58.

48   Pali Jae Lee and Koko Willis, *Tales from the Night Rainbow* (Night Rainbow Publishing Co., 1990), 24.

49   Daniel Kikawa, *Perpetuated in Righteousness* (Keaʻau, HI: Aloha Ke Akua Publishing, 1994), 144-145.

50   Daniel Kikawa, *Perpetuated in Righteousness* (Keaʻau, HI: Aloha Ke Akua Publishing, 1994), 153-154.

51   Daniel Kikawa, *Perpetuated in Righteousness* (Keaʻau, HI: Aloha Ke Akua Publishing, 1994), 168.

52   1 Nephi 4:2.

53 President Russell M. Nelson, "The Price of Priesthood Power," *General Conference*, April 2016.

54 Terry Pratchett, *I Shall Wear Midnight* (New York: HarperCollins, 2010), 184.

55 Kahikahealani Wight, Professor of Hawaiian Language and Literature, Kapi'olani Community College.

56 Dino Labiste.

57 Boyd K. Packer quoted in David A. Bednar, *Act in Doctrine* (Salt Lake City, UT: Deseret Book, 2012), 134.

58 Doctrine and Covenants 84:88.

59 Psalm 91:11-12, Doctrine and Covenants 103:20.

60 Matthew 4:11, Joseph Smith Translation.

61 Moroni 10:8-19.

62 Orson Pratt, *Journal of Discourses,* Volume 25, 146.

63 Moroni 10:30.

64 Doctrine and Covenants 46:8.

65 Job 8:10, New Living Translation.

66 M.J. Harden, *Voices of Wisdom: Hawaiian Elders Speak* (Kula, HI: Aka Press, 1999), 56.

67 Pali Jae Lee and Koko Willis, *Tales from the Night Rainbow* (Night Rainbow Publishing Co., 1990), 108.

68 Alma 8:14-15.

69 President Brigham Young confirmed that the spirit world "Is on this earth." (*Discourses of Brigham Young*, 376). President Ezra Taft Benson declared that "the spirit world is not far away. Sometimes the veil between this life and the life beyond becomes very thin. Our loved ones who have passed on are not far from us." (*Ensign*, June 1971, 33.).

70 Moses 1:10.

71 "We could think people home. We sent messages to them wherever they might be and have them come home if we needed them." (Pali Jae Lee and Koko Willis, *Tales from the Night Rainbow* (Night Rainbow Publishing Co., 1990), 59).

72 Psalm 43:3, King James Version.

73 Psalm 43:3, New International Version.

74 Psalm 43:4, New International Version.

75 1 Nephi 18:16.

76 2 Nephi 31:13.

77 Ether 6:9.

78 Mark 9:23, Evangelical Heritage Version.

79 Kaili'ohe Kame'ekua lived in Kamalo, Moloka'i from 1816–1931. Kaili'ohe shared her experience witnessing her kumu (teachers) travel by faith saying, "We were excited about our lessons. There was so much to learn… We took trips into the mountains and by the sea shore. These trips were loved by all. We would practice our chanting as we journeyed. On more than one occasion, we would leave in the company of one of the older, more experienced

students, leaving our teacher behind in meditation, and then find her waiting for us at the seashore or at a certain spot high on the mountain top. I knew nothing was impossible, and I cannot say I was surprised." (Pali Jae Lee and Koko Willis, *Tales from the Night Rainbow* (Night Rainbow Publishing Co., 1990), 46).

80   "The things which are impossible with men are possible with God." Luke 18:27. "All things are possible to him that believeth." Mark 9:23.

81   Pali Jae Lee and Koko Willis, *Tales from the Night Rainbow* (Night Rainbow Publishing Co., 1990), 53.

82   Matthew 17:20.

83   Doctrine and Covenants 59:20.

84   Researchers have been unable to discover how the moai (large human figures carved from stone) of Easter Island were moved. Researchers have tended to assume that the statues were dragged somehow, using a lot of ropes and wood. One of the island locals responded to these ideas of the researchers saying, "The experts can say whatever they want but we know the truth." In the Rapanui oral tradition, the moai were moved by mana, a spiritual force transmitted by powerful ancestors. Retrieved February 5, 2016 from http://ngm.nationalgeographic.com/2012/07/easter-island/bloch-text?source=news_easter_island_story.

85   Matthew 14:22–31, King James Version.

86   Matthew 10:5–8, King James Version.

87   John 14:12-13, King James Version.

88   Matthew 14:29, King James Version.

89   Mark 16:17–18, King James Version.

90   Mark 9:23, King James 2000 Bible.

91   Acts 6:8, King James Version.

92   John 6:16-21, New King James Version.

93   John 6:21, New King James Version.

94   Similar to the words found in Joshua 3:5.

95   Matthew 9:20-22.

96   Mark 6:56, King James Version.

97   Mark 3:10, New International Version.

98   Luke 6:19, King James 2000 Bible.

99   Matthew 14:35-36, New International Version.

100   Matthew 26:39.

101   Luke 22:44; D&C 19:18; Russell M. Nelson, "Why This Holy Land?" *Ensign*, December 1989, 17–18.

102   2 Timothy 3:5, King James Version

103   President Russell M. Nelson, "Ministering with the Power and Authority of God," *General Conference*, April 2018.

104   Matthew 17:14-21.

105   *Autobiography of Parley P. Pratt*, ed. Scot Facer Proctor and Maurine Jensen Proctor, rev. and enhanced ed. (Salt Lake City: Deseret Book, 2000), 355.

106   Wilford Woodruff, *Wilford Woodruff, His Life and Labors*, comp. Matthias F. Cowley, 104-106.

107   Acts 19:11-12, New International Version.

108   Edward L. Kimball, *Lengthen Your Stride: The Presidency of Spencer W. Kimball* (Salt Lake City, UT: Deseret Book, 2005), 54-55.

109   2 Nephi 25:26.

110   Retrieved from http://www.americanforests.org/big-trees/palm-coconut-cocos-nucifera/.

111   Jeremiah 2:13, New Century Version.

112   "The Son of Righteousness shall appear unto them; and he shall heal them, and they shall have peace with him." 2 Nephi 26:9.

113   "Blessed are those who hunger and thirst for righteousness, for they will be filled." Matthew 5:6, New International Version.

114   "O have mercy, and apply the atoning blood of Christ that I may receive forgiveness of my sins." Mosiah 4:2.

115   John 7:37, King James Version.

116   John 4:14, New International Version.

117   John 3:16-17, King James Version.

118   Doctrine and Covenants 78:18.

119   2 Corinthians 6:2b, Good News Translation.

120   Matthew 21:1-17; Mark 11:1-11; Luke 19:29-40; John 12:12-19.

121   John 12:12-13.

122   Luke 19:37.

123   Matthew 21:9.

124   John 12:13, Luke 19:38.

125   Mark 11:10.

126   John 7:37.

127   Isaiah 12:3, GOD'S WORD Translation.

128   John 7:37-38, King James Version.

129   Isaiah 44:3, King James Version.

130   Bruce R. McConkie, *Doctrinal New Testament Commentary, Volume 1* (Salt Lake City, Utah: Bookcraft, 1974), 445-446.

131   3 Nephi 11:17.

132   "Know ye not that ye are the temple of God?" 1 Corinthians 3:16, King James Version.

133   Doctrine and Covenants 62:23.

134   Matthew 5:6, New International Version.

135   Russell M. Nelson, *The Gateway We Call Death* (Salt Lake City, UT: Deseret Book, 1995), 24.

136   Psalm 46:10, King James Version.

137   Mark 4:39, King James Version.

138   Psalm 23:1-3, King James Version.

139   Jesus "departed again into a mountain himself alone." John 6:15.
      Jesus "departed into a mountain to pray." Mark 6:46.

Jesus "went out into a mountain to pray, and continued all night in prayer to God." Luke 6:12.

"When [Jesus] had sent the multitudes away, he went up into a mountain apart to pray: and when the evening was come, he was there alone." Matthew 14:23.

140   Mark 6:31, New International Version.

141   Nephi 18:3.

142   Max Lucado, *Max on Life* (Nashville, TN: Thomas Nelson, 2010), 79.

143   Psalm 34:2, The Message.

144   John H. Groberg, *The Other Side of Heaven* (Salt Lake City: UT: Deseret Book Company, 1993), 114.

145   President David O. McKay, *Conference Report*, April 1967, General Priesthood Meeting, 85.

146   Exodus 14:14, New International Version.

147   Helaman 5:30.

148   1 Timothy 6:21, The Living Bible.

149   "The Lord Jesus Christ…is or should be our best Friend." (Bruce R. McConkie, "Our Relationship with the Lord," *BYU Devotional*, March 2, 1982).

150   John 17:3, King James Version.

151   Alma 23:5-6.

152   D. Todd Christofferson, "Why the Church," *General Conference*, October 2015.

153   3 Nephi 28:23.

154   Matthew 25:1-11, Joseph Smith Translation.

155   Thomas Kinkade, *Lightposts for Living* (New York: Warner Books, 1999), viii.

156   Van James, *Ancient Sites of Maui, Molokaʻi, and Lānaʻi* (Honolulu, HI: Mutual Publishing, 2001), 143-145.

157   1 Samuel 16:7, King James Version.

158   Doctrine and Covenants 33:8.

159   Catherine Cluett, "Kalaupapa Barge Day," *Molokaʻi Dispatch*, July 17, 2013.

160   Luke 9:58, New King James Version.

161   Jan de Volder, *The Spirit of Father Damien* (San Francisco: Ignatius Press, 2010), 7.

162   John Beevers, *A Man for Now* (Garden City, NY: Doubleday & Company, Inc., 1973), 23.

163   Jan de Volder, *The Spirit of Father Damien* (San Francisco: Ignatius Press, 2010), 10.

164   John Beevers, *A Man for Now* (Garden City, NY: Doubleday & Company, Inc., 1973), 30.

165   John Beevers, *A Man for Now* (Garden City, NY: Doubleday & Company, Inc., 1973), 42.

166   *National Park Service*. Retrieved April 16, 2014 from http://www.nps.gov/kala/historyculture/words.htm.

167   *National Park Service*. Retrieved April 16, 2014 from http://www.nps.gov/kala/historyculture/words.htm.

168 John Beevers, *A Man for Now* (Garden City, NY: Doubleday & Company, Inc., 1973), 57-58.

169 John Beevers, *A Man for Now* (Garden City, NY: Doubleday & Company, Inc., 1973), 59.

170 John Beevers, *A Man for Now* (Garden City, NY: Doubleday & Company, Inc., 1973), 62.

171 Isaiah 6:8, King James Version.

172 John Beevers, *A Man for Now* (Garden City, NY: Doubleday & Company, Inc., 1973), 63.

173 Luke 9:58, New King James Version.

174 Matthew 20:28, King James Version.

175 Mark 9:33–35, King James Version.

176 Briner and Pritchard, *Leadership Lessons of Jesus*, 293–294.

177 Matthew 23:11, King James Version.

178 Luke 22:42, King James Version.

179 Jan de Volder, *The Spirit of Father Damien* (San Francisco: Ignatius Press, 2010), 43, 23.

180 John Beevers, *A Man for Now* (Garden City, NY: Doubleday & Company, Inc., 1973), 109.

181 Jan de Volder, *The Spirit of Father Damien* (San Francisco: Ignatius Press, 2010), 7.

182 Jan de Volder, *The Spirit of Father Damien* (San Francisco: Ignatius Press, 2010), 50.

183 Jan de Volder, *The Spirit of Father Damien* (San Francisco: Ignatius Press, 2010), 54-55.

184 John Beevers, *A Man for Now* (Garden City, NY: Doubleday & Company, Inc., 1973), 69-70.

185 Jan de Volder, *The Spirit of Father Damien* (San Francisco: Ignatius Press, 2010), 50.

186 John Beevers, *A Man for Now* (Garden City, NY: Doubleday & Company, Inc., 1973), 77.

187 Luke 2:40, 52.

188 Russell M. Nelson, *Accomplishing the Impossible* (Salt Lake City, UT: Deseret Book, 2015), 121-122.

189 David A. Bednar, "Quick to Observe," *BYU Devotional*, May 10, 2005.

190 John Tayman, *The Colony* (New York, NY: A Lisa Drew Book/Scribner, 2006), 127.
Jan de Volder, *The Spirit of Father Damien* (San Francisco: Ignatius Press, 2010), 73.

191 John Beevers, *A Man for Now* (Garden City, NY: Doubleday & Company, Inc., 1973), 95.

192 Jan de Volder, *The Spirit of Father Damien* (San Francisco: Ignatius Press, 2010), 67.

193 Acts 10:34, King James Version.

194   John Beevers, *A Man for Now* (Garden City, NY: Doubleday & Company, Inc., 1973), 14.

195   1 Peter 1:3, King James Version.

196   Alma 31:5.

197   "In the beginning was the Word, and the Word was with God, and the Word was God." John 1:1, King James Version.

198   1 Nephi 11:25.

199   John Beevers, *A Man for Now* (Garden City, NY: Doubleday & Company, Inc., 1973), 66.

200   Jan de Volder, *The Spirit of Father Damien* (San Francisco: Ignatius Press, 2010), 36.

201   Jan de Volder, *The Spirit of Father Damien* (San Francisco: Ignatius Press, 2010), 36-37.

202   John Beevers, *A Man for Now* (Garden City, NY: Doubleday & Company, Inc., 1973), 67.

203   Jan de Volder, *The Spirit of Father Damien* (San Francisco: Ignatius Press, 2010), 58.

204   John Beevers, *A Man for Now* (Garden City, NY: Doubleday & Company, Inc., 1973), 74.

205   3 Nephi 11:15.

206   3 Nephi 17:21.

207   3 Nephi 18:36.

208   Helaman 16:22.

209   Jan de Volder, *The Spirit of Father Damien* (San Francisco: Ignatius Press, 2010), 68.

210   Luke 23:24, King James Version.

211   Gordon B. Hinckley, "Of You It Is Required to Forgive," *Ensign*, June 1991.

212   John 15:20, King James Version.

213   Matthew 5:11-12, King James Version.

214   Exodus 14:14, New International Version.

215   Russell M. Nelson, *Accomplishing the Impossible* (Salt Lake City, UT: Deseret Book, 2015), 12.

216   Jan de Volder, *The Spirit of Father Damien* (San Francisco: Ignatius Press, 2010), 146.

217   Jan de Volder, *The Spirit of Father Damien* (San Francisco: Ignatius Press, 2010), 149-150.

218   John Beevers, *A Man for Now* (Garden City, NY: Doubleday & Company, Inc., 1973), 133.

219   Jan de Volder, *The Spirit of Father Damien* (San Francisco: Ignatius Press, 2010), 61.

220   John Beevers, *A Man for Now* (Garden City, NY: Doubleday & Company, Inc., 1973), 74.

221   Jan de Volder, *The Spirit of Father Damien* (San Francisco: Ignatius Press, 2010), 68-69.

222 John Beevers, *A Man for Now* (Garden City, NY: Doubleday & Company, Inc., 1973), 85-86.

223 1 Peter 5:5, New King James Version.

224 John Beevers, *A Man for Now* (Garden City, NY: Doubleday & Company, Inc., 1973), 154.

225 John Beevers, *A Man for Now* (Garden City, NY: Doubleday & Company, Inc., 1973), 169.

226 Russell M. Nelson, *Accomplishing the Impossible* (Salt Lake City, UT: Deseret Book, 2015), 2.

227 1 Corinthians 1:26-28, New International Version.

228 Jan de Volder, *The Spirit of Father Damien* (San Francisco: Ignatius Press, 2010), 82.

229 Jan de Volder, *The Spirit of Father Damien* (San Francisco: Ignatius Press, 2010), 135-136.

230 Jan de Volder, *The Spirit of Father Damien* (San Francisco: Ignatius Press, 2010), 152.

231 John Beevers, *A Man for Now* (Garden City, NY: Doubleday & Company, Inc., 1973), 83.

232 John Beevers, *A Man for Now* (Garden City, NY: Doubleday & Company, Inc., 1973), 108.
Pat Williams, Jim Denney, *How to Be Like Jesus* (Deerfield Beach, FL: Faith Communications, 2003), 378-379.

233 Jan de Volder, *The Spirit of Father Damien* (San Francisco: Ignatius Press, 2010), 108.

234 Jan de Volder, *The Spirit of Father Damien* (San Francisco: Ignatius Press, 2010), 141-142.

235 John Beevers, *A Man for Now* (Garden City, NY: Doubleday & Company, Inc., 1973), 134.

236 Jan de Volder, *The Spirit of Father Damien* (San Francisco: Ignatius Press, 2010), 153.
John Beevers, *A Man for Now* (Garden City, NY: Doubleday & Company, Inc., 1973), 139.

237 Jan de Volder, *The Spirit of Father Damien* (San Francisco: Ignatius Press, 2010), 154.

238 Jan de Volder, *The Spirit of Father Damien* (San Francisco: Ignatius Press, 2010), 151.

239 Jan de Volder, *The Spirit of Father Damien* (San Francisco: Ignatius Press, 2010), 154.

240 "The fruit of the Spirit is love, joy, peace, longsuffering, gentleness, goodness, faith, meekness, temperance." Galatians 5:22-23, King James Version.

241 Matthew 10:39, English Standard Version.

242 Jan de Volder, *The Spirit of Father Damien* (San Francisco: Ignatius Press, 2010), 126.

243 Doctrine and Covenants 52:14.

244 Jan de Volder, *The Spirit of Father Damien* (San Francisco: Ignatius Press, 2010), 112.

245 Jan de Volder, *The Spirit of Father Damien* (San Francisco: Ignatius Press, 2010, 115.

246 Joshua 4:21:24, King James Version.

247 John 12:36, King James Version.

248 Pali Jae Lee and Koko Willis, *Tales from the Night Rainbow* (Night Rainbow Publishing Co., 1990), 101-103.

249 John 2:1-10, King James Version.

250 Psalm 135:3, King James Version.

251 Hawaiian for "Praise the Lord."

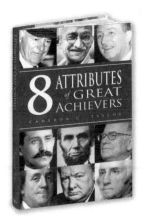

8 Attributes of Great Achievers

"I thought *8 Attributes of Great Achievers* was an excellent read with interesting and deep stories. I enjoyed it more than any book I've read in quite a while. I had a hard time putting it down."

-MARK DENNISON

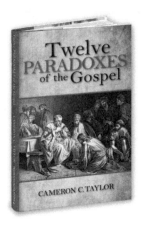

Twelve Paradoxes of the Gospel

"Cameron's strong faith comes through in his book and there is no doubt he was inspired to write it."

-LOU HOLTZ, Former Head Football Coach, *University of Notre Dame*

Preserve, Protect & Defend

"*Preserve, Protect & Defend* was a great read, filled with the spirit all through. No man wrote it, God did. I'm 61 and cried all through it. Thank you for sharing your talents."

-S. DEAN CHAPPELL

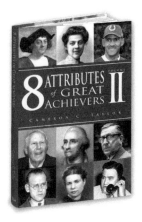

8 Attributes of Great Achievers Volume II

"I am writing to share with you how much I enjoyed reading your book. I was deeply touched, encouraged, inspired, and challenged. I laughed and I cried. Every day I have been sharing with my husband what I am learning, and I keep on saying 'This is such an amazing book!!!'"

-CORA BUSHEY

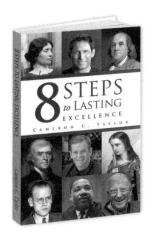

8 Steps to Lasting Excellence

"Phenomenal. I devoured this book in 3 days, as the stories, lessons, and insights proved amazing."

-CHRISTOPHER WILD

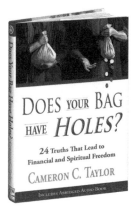

Does Your Bag Have Holes?

"Cameron was meant to write, and he does so beautifully. He writes with humor, insight, and profound wisdom. I came across so many different stories that I wanted to scan/type in and share. They're that amazing."

-JOI SIGERS

Available at: www.CameronCTaylor.com